PLANTS FROM PLANTS

The Secrets of Propagating More Than 60 Different Kinds of Houseplants for Next to Nothing

by Suzanne Crayson

Illustrated by the Author

J. B. LIPPINCOTT COMPANY

Philadelphia and New York

U.S. Library of Congress Cataloging in Publication Data

Crayson, Suzanne, birth date
    Plants from plants.

    Includes index.
        1. House plants.   2. Plant propagation.
I. Title.
SB419.C66   635.9'65   76-12559
ISBN-0-397-01175-X (pbk.)

For my dear old dad

CONTENTS

INTRODUCTION

This book is about plant propagation: the creation of new plants from existing ones. I had always wanted a houseful of plants but could never afford more than a few, so I decided that I would learn to propagate my own plants and thus save a lot of money.

I studied plant book after plant book, which told me everything I needed to know about buying, watering, caring for and feeding my plants but very little about multiplying them. I went to the library to find the kind of reference books nurserymen might use, but I became very confused because I couldn't understand the Greek or Latin terms. It was then I realized that I would have to learn about plant propagation on my own.

This book is the result of my trials and errors over the years. Experience has been my only teacher, and I would like to pass on to you some of the lessons I have learned. What I have tried to do in this book is to give you detailed, step-by-step instructions for each houseplant, written in language you can understand.

The most important thing you will learn from this book is that, by propagating your own plants, you can multiply them tenfold so that, by judicious swapping with your friends, you can achieve a plant collection that rivals a plant store. *And all this at practically no cost.*

Now don't expect it all to be clear sailing—you are bound to have your failures. The thing is to try not to become too discouraged when this happens—you aren't God and plants sometimes die.

Remember that a plant is a living thing. We are all living things, and we respond to love and attention in the same way. If you treat your plants with kindness, anticipation and respect, they will do their best to please you in return.

EQUIPMENT

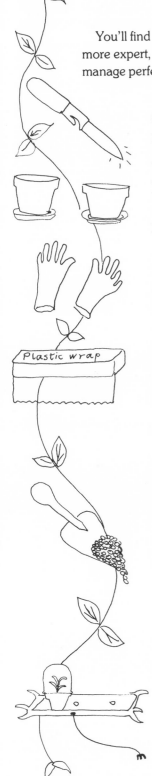

You'll find a lot of your gardening tools right in your own kitchen. As you become more expert, you may want to buy additional equipment; but until then you can manage perfectly well with the items listed below.

Sharp knife   Always sterilize it before use by wiping it with alcohol. This will prevent bacterial transfer from plant to plant.

Crocks   These are what your flowerpots become after you drop them. (See page 4, "Crocking Your Pots.")

Empty jars and bottles   Use the bottles to root cuttings in water; wide-mouthed jars serve as individual greenhouses. (See page 7, "Humidity.")

Flowerpots   Start out with a few and buy more as you need them. If the pots will be sitting on furniture, buy saucers to match.

Fungicide   This is a powder used to prevent root rot.

Growing mediums   Potting soil, vermiculite, mosses and sand. (See pages 2–3.)

Hormone powder   Apply to cut ends to encourage rooting.

Plastic wraps   Buy a roll of plastic wrap and save everything from Baggies to cleaning bags.

Props   Bamboo or plastic stakes can be bought in various lengths. Twigs or chopsticks can often be used as substitutes.

Trowel   A kitchen spoon or tablespoon will also do.

Twist-ems   Made just for gardening, these are longer than the ones that come with rolls of plastic bags.

Vitamin B$_1$ (thiamine hydrochloride)   A root stimulant which is an effective antishock treatment, it is sold in garden centers under various trade names.

Watering can   Get one with a long, thin spout.

Watering guides   These gadgets which you can buy at plant shops let you know when your plant needs watering.

Water mister   This provides humidity for your plant.

Yogurt maker   This provides the best way to get a constant source of mild bottom heat. (See page 9, "Temperature.")

Confidence   It comes with experience!

GROWING MEDIUMS

WATER

Water is the easiest rooting medium of all, and it's fun to see the roots growing. You can root almost anything in water provided that you have good light. Cuttings root much faster in small bottles, perhaps because they are able to get oxygen more easily from smaller amounts of water. They take from one day to one month to form roots. Place a small piece of charcoal in the water to keep it from becoming slimy. Be sure to top up the water level daily, as it evaporates quickly. When roots have formed, the cuttings can be planted directly in potting soil.

The only disadvantage to rooting cuttings in water is that the roots formed are much finer than those formed in vermiculite, with the result that a water-rooted cutting often suffers from shock when it is transferred to soil. To avoid wilting, water the cutting with a solution of vitamin B_1, which is an antishock treatment, and give it the "greenhouse treatment" for a few days. (See page 7, "Humidity," for instructions on how to create a greenhouse.)

VERMICULITE

Vermiculite is another good rooting medium for your cuttings. It is a gray "soilless" medium made from mica which looks and acts just like Kitty Litter (for which it can be substituted in an emergency). It is used for rooting young plants, but it is not recommended for mature plants because it contains no nutrients. Vermiculite can be used over and over again, as it is sterile.

Vermiculite's main characteristic is that it absorbs large quantities of water without turning soggy. This can cause problems when it is used in plastic pots, which do not allow evaporation through their sides. Algae may form on the surface of the vermiculite, which is an indication that your cutting is not getting enough oxygen and is in danger of suffocating. However, this problem does not occur when vermiculite is used in clay pots.

To prepare vermiculite, pour it into a plastic basin and gradually add water until it has reached full absorption and no longer flies up when you shake the basin. Spoon it into a clean flowerpot whose bottom hole is covered with a crock. Next, take the base of a spare pot and gently press down on the mixture. This squeezes out some of the water and makes the vermiculite shrink to half its volume. Add more vermiculite and squeeze until the flowerpot is full. This creates a firm base to hold your cutting upright. Now take a stick and make a hole in the center of the vermiculite. Place your cutting in the hole and press gently around the stem with your fingers.

Whether you use an individual flowerpot, a cutting pot or a seed box, the method for preparing vermiculite is always the same and is the technique used whenever I tell you to "fill a pot with prepared vermiculite."

POTTING SOIL

Commercially prepared potting soil is a mixture of soil, humus and sand with added nutrients. It is pasteurized and sterilized, and it provides an excellent growing medium for all young plants after they have formed roots. For most plants it can be used straight from the bag with no further preparation.

SPECIAL SOILS

Certain plants require special soils—from cacti, which grow best in a quick-draining soil, to African violets, which grow best in a water-retentive soil. To create these special soil mixtures, add one of the following.

SAND

Both horticultural sand from your nursery and clean builder's sand should be sterilized by pouring boiling water over it. Sea sand is tempting because it is free, but restrain yourself as it is far too salty and will kill your plants. Sand is used in a soil recipe to make the soil more porous. I always use sand when rooting cuttings in plastic pots.

MOSSES

Green moss and sphagnum moss can be used interchangeably. They come in bags and should be soaked in water and wrung out before use. These mosses are used for lining wire hanging baskets, for air layering plants, and for rooting plants that do not grow in soil. They also act as a fungicide when used as a top layer over seeds.

Peat moss is partly decomposed sphagnum moss, used for plants that need acidity and a water-retentive soil. It takes the place of leaf mold or humus, soils made from decomposed leaves, which are hard to find unless you live in the country—or have your own compost heap.

USED SOIL

It is not necessary to throw away used soil, as it can be reused. When you have accumulated enough to fill a large brown-paper supermarket bag (double two bags for extra strength), place the bag with soil in a roasting pan, and gradually add a pint of water. Tie the top of the bag with string and place it in the oven set at the lowest temperature. Let it cook for three hours with the kitchen door closed, as it smells rather strange. The water evaporates into steam and penetrates the soil, killing off any spores, which are microorganisms in a dormant state. If you don't kill off these spores, they will return to life later and attack your plant. That is why using ordinary garden soil can be a bit risky unless you sterilize it first.

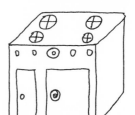

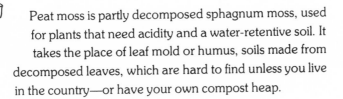

3

PREPARING YOUR POTS

TYPES OF POTS

You have a choice of clay, ceramic or plastic pots, available in all sizes. A three-inch pot is a good size for a new cutting. I use clay pots whenever possible because clay is porous and allows the cutting to "breathe." Plastic pots are nonporous; when used in conjunction with vermiculite, algae often form on the surface and suffocate the cutting.

As a compromise, I use sand when rooting cuttings in plastic pots and vermiculite when rooting cuttings in clay pots. There are times when plastic pots are an advantage: for hanging plants (because a plastic pot is much lighter than clay) and for plants that must be kept damp at all times (because water in a plastic pot evaporates twice as slowly as water in a clay pot). A rule to remember, therefore, is that you should water plants in clay pots twice as often as those in plastic pots.

A decorative ceramic pot, if it has a hole in the bottom, can be used in place of a clay pot. If there is no hole, it is an ornamental container for a flowerpot, known as a "cache pot" (from the French, meaning "to hide the pot").

WASHING OUT YOUR POTS

All pots can be used over and over again. In between use you must wash them thoroughly in very hot water to which you have added a dash of household bleach. Use a scrubbing brush to remove every speck of dirt. Rinse and dry.

If your plant has died, you would be well advised to boil its pot in a bucket of water on top of the stove. This will kill off any spores or bacteria the diseased plant may have left. Since plastic melts when boiled, I would advise throwing away both the plant and its pot if your plant has died in a plastic pot of causes other than overwatering or underwatering.

CROCKING YOUR POTS

Crocks are pieces of broken flowerpots large enough to cover the bottom hole of the pot. Crocking prevents the roots from growing out of the bottom hole and stops water from running out of the bottom hole onto your feet. Also, it gives the roots something to hold on to. You should always crock your pot whether you are filling it with vermiculite, sand or potting soil. Put in one or two pieces and overlap them so that the bottom hole is covered.

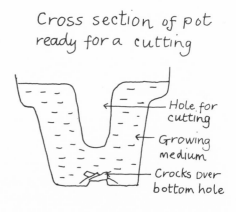

Cross section of pot ready for a cutting

Hole for cutting

Growing medium

Crocks over bottom hole

Because plastic pots have several holes, cover the bottom holes with pebbles.

SPECIAL CONTAINERS

Most cuttings can be rooted in a bottle of water or a small pot filled with vermiculite. However, there are other kinds of containers which are useful in special circumstances.

PEAT POTS

These pots are available in many garden centers, but I seldom use them for indoor gardening because they dry out so rapidly. However, when using a "two-stage" pot, they are invaluable.

"TWO-STAGE" POT

The "two-stage" pot is used when rooting fragile-stemmed cuttings that always break upon transfer to soil. A peat pot filled with vermiculite is inserted into a large bulb pot filled with potting soil. The cuttings form roots in the vermiculite and grow through the sides of the peat pot into the potting soil. (For use, see page 39.)

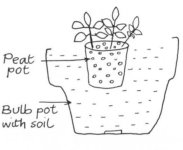

Peat pot

Bulb pot with soil

"Two-stage" pot

"CAKE-PAN" POT

The "cake-pan" pot is used when rooting African violet and peperomia leaves. The water in the small clay pot seeps through its sides into the vermiculite in the large bulb pot, thus keeping it constantly damp. This pot can be used for any cuttings that have to be kept moist and is particularly useful if you are going away for a few days and are worried that the vermiculite may dry out. (For use, see page 18.)

Leaves

Clay pot with water

Hole plugged with chewing gum

"Cake-pan" pot

Seed box filled with vermiculite

SEED BOXES

Seed boxes are useful when you have a lot of cuttings. They can be bought very cheaply from your local garden center, where they are used to grow plants from seed. (For use, see page 52.)

THE CARE OF
YOUR CUTTINGS

Cuttings require special care. During their first weeks of life their requirements regarding water, light, humidity and temperature are quite different from their requirements as mature plants.

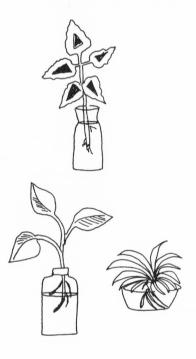

WATER

Cuttings must be kept moist at all times in order to form roots, and one reason vermiculite is such a good growing medium is that it has an ability to retain moisture. Cuttings that are rooting in tiny two- to three-inch pots need to be checked daily to make sure that the vermiculite isn't drying out.

A good rule to remember is that *cuttings in small pots require watering twice as often as those in large pots.* This rule applies whether your growing medium is vermiculite, sand or soil. Stick your finger into the vermiculite and feel if it is wet or dry. If the pot feels very light, you can be sure that the vermiculite will be dry because a pot of vermiculite is only as heavy as the amount of water it has absorbed.

To repeat: Don't rely on your mature plant's requirements when caring for its offspring. Even a geranium that is kept on the dry side when mature needs to be kept on the moist side when a baby.

LIGHT

Cuttings will root twice as fast in bright light; therefore, if you have a window facing south or west, you will get better results than if your window is facing north or east. Although cuttings do not need direct sunshine falling on their leaves, they need brightness, and this is perhaps why the artificial plant lights are so successful. These lights provide a controlled intensity of light, never too strong for the growing plants, and you can control the length of their days by turning them off earlier or later.

So if your home has only one window, which faces north, and you have a twenty-story building going up across the street, do not despair! You may find that your best rooting takes place on the floor of your darkest cupboard—with a plant light.

A plant light is available either as a bulb which fits into a holder or as a wide-spectrum fluorescent tube which fits into a desk lamp.

Because my only good windowsill faces east and the results I had been getting weren't very good, I tried an experiment rooting cuttings in a cupboard with a plant light and comparing results. The cuttings in the cupboard all rooted within one week, whereas the cuttings on the windowsill took a month, and one of them (the schefflera) refused to root at all. So if you want to make life easier for yourself for a very modest cost, invest in a plant light.

HUMIDITY

The "greenhouse effect" is created when plants are placed in an enclosed space where they are protected from the outside air. In its simplest form, the greenhouse is created by putting a plastic bag over a plant. The bag should be held up by a prop such as a chopstick which is stuck into the vermiculite. Try not to let the bag touch the leaves. For a larger plant, reverse the bag and tie it under the rim of the pot with string.

Moisture forms on the inside of the bag within a few hours. Plants are able to absorb moisture through their leaves as well as through their roots, and this enables them to survive when their roots have been injured.

You can control the amount of moisture required inside the greenhouse by making small tears in the plastic bag, allowing some mingling of the outside and inside air. If mist does not form, it is because the growing medium is too dry.

Use a greenhouse for the following reasons:

1. Cuttings rooted in vermiculite. They will survive the initial shock of being severed far better if their leaves are bathed in moisture.

2. Transferring a rooted cutting from water to soil. Almost without exception, a plant will wilt from shock when its fine roots try to adjust from water to the comparative dryness of the soil. A week in the greenhouse will help a young plant's leaves absorb enough moisture to survive until the roots have recovered sufficiently to take over. If you water your plant with a vitamin B_1 solution for the first week after transferring from water to soil, it will recover more rapidly.

3. Plants off-color. If your plant seems to be going into a decline for no apparent reason, a week in a greenhouse will affect it as if it had had a trip to a health spa.

Other forms of individual greenhouses are jam jars, plastic ice-cream containers and plastic drinking glasses. These all balance on the rim of the flowerpot and can be tilted a little if the moisture buildup inside becomes too heavy.

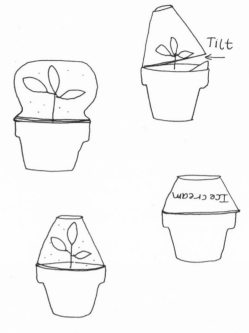

Transparent bread box good for rooting single leaves

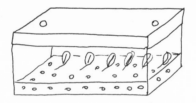

A greenhouse for a group of cuttings can be made out of a plastic bread box with a tight-fitting lid. Two inches of prepared vermiculite on the bottom provide the growing medium. If too much moisture builds up on the sides of the box, make one or two holes in the top with a screwdriver heated over a gas flame.

WARNING: HARDENING UP

The greenhouse provides a wonderful womblike atmosphere for your young plant; but the time always comes when the little fellow has to face the cold world on the outside, and this takes acclimatization. This must be done *very slowly* or your plant will wilt and die.

If your greenhouse is a plastic bag, open up the small tears little by little until the bag is ripped apart. If you are using individual jars, tilt them a little more each day until there is an inch of space through which the outside air can mix with that inside. If using a plastic bread box, slowly lift up the lid.

The hardening-up process may take as long as five days, so don't try to rush it. At the first sign of wilting, restore the greenhouse quickly and start again more slowly.

The term "hardening up" refers to this process of acclimatizing the plant inside the greenhouse to the colder air outside. "Toughening up" might be a more apt term.

TEMPERATURE

Cuttings do very well in temperatures from 60 to 80 degrees Fahrenheit, just like their parents. The term "bottom heat" is often repeated in this book when dealing with stem cuttings and offsets, and it refers to providing heat underneath the plant to encourage rooting.

Professional gardeners put together complicated, expensive contraptions of wires and switches to obtain this magical condition, but I have a much better suggestion: a yogurt maker. It produces a constant source of warmth, provided by a couple of low-watt light bulbs under a metal or plastic tray, and the amount of heat required to turn milk into yogurt seems to be the identical amount needed by cuttings to form roots.

A cutting receiving bottom heat should always be put into an individual greenhouse or else the growing medium will dry out immediately.

If your cutting is in a very small pot, stand it on a layer of pebbles placed on top of the yogurt maker. This will prevent it from getting too warm.

After four to six weeks on the yogurt maker and in a greenhouse, your cutting will have rooted. It is necessary to remove it from the heat first and then, a day or so later, to start the hardening-up process by slowly removing the greenhouse atmosphere.

FERTILIZATION

You don't have to worry about fertilizing your cuttings during their first two months because they don't need it. Just use the vitamin B_1 solution as an antishock treatment for the first week and plain water thereafter. However, when they have rooted and it is time to put them in potting soil, they will benefit from being fertilized.

Be sure to use your fertilizer at a quarter-strength to begin with as you don't want to burn the young roots. And since you water plants in small pots more frequently, *make the mixture weaker for those in smaller pots than for those in larger pots.*

POTTING YOUR CUTTINGS

After your cutting has developed roots in vermiculite, it is time to move him into soil. Crock a small pot—a round or square four-inch pot is a good size at this stage—and put an inch of potting soil into its bottom.

Gently remove the cutting from its old container, shake off as much vermiculite as you can from the root ball, and put it into its new pot. Carefully hold the cutting with one hand and fill in the space around it with potting soil with your other hand. Keep adding soil until it is an inch from the rim. Press the soil gently around the cutting and give the pot a couple of bangs to settle the soil and eliminate any air pockets.

Now water your young plant with vitamin B₁ as an antishock treatment and wish him well! He will stay in this pot until he is mature and ready for "potting up." (See page 113.)

PINCHING BACK

Your plant can be pinched back as soon as he is more than six inches in height. What is called "pruning" to a tree is called "pinching back" to a young plant. It is a term that describes removing the top leaves to encourage branching and promote growth lower down.

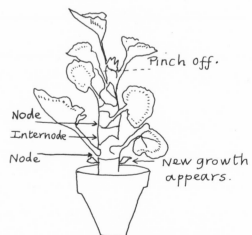

With your finger and thumb pinch off the new leaves at the top of the stem. You may feel like a murderer, so remember that you are actually helping the plant become bushier, thicker and more beautiful.

Plants such as coleus, wandering Jew and ivy need to be pinched back regularly to force them to branch out. This is a very good way to obtain new material for cuttings! Fuchsias benefit from being pinched back as soon as they have eight sets of leaves; the tips can be rooted in water to form new plants, as long as they have at least *three nodes*. A node is the place from which the leaves grow. The area between two nodes is called the "internode."

DIFFERENT METHODS
OF PROPAGATION

STEM-TIP CUTTINGS

The easiest method of propagation is to make stem-tip cuttings, known to our grandparents as "slips." These cuttings are the four-inch tips of stems containing at least three nodes. They form roots in plain water or vermiculite; when potted in soil, they become plants exactly like their parents.

Some plants that give good stem-tip cuttings are geranium, coleus, pothos and wandering Jew.

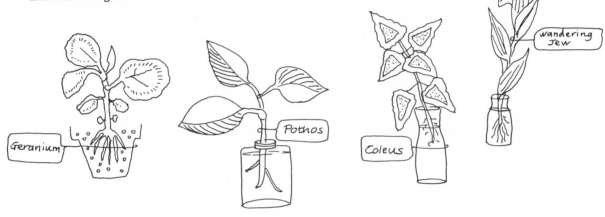

OFFSETS

In this category, found under the general heading of offsets, are "offshoots," "stolons," "suckers" and "runners." These are the tiny, but complete, plants which grow by the side of, or on top of, the mother plant.

Chinese evergreen and dracaena put out suckers at the base of the mother plant, and these suckers can be cut away with some of her roots.

The spider plant and the strawberry geranium put out runners which hang on long stems below the mother plant and which can be rooted in small pots while still attached to the mother.

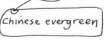

"Hen and chicks" and prickly pear grow off the mother plant and can be cut off to form a new plant.

DIVISION

When a plant becomes too big to handle, you have to divide it into two or more smaller ones. Plants that can be divided are those which form "crowns" at the soil level and do not grow from a central stem. If you remove a mature African violet from its pot, you will see that it is actually made up of three or four smaller crowns, each one a potential plant. The roots should be gently pried apart and cut.

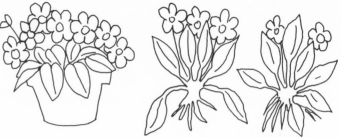

Ferns are divided in half.

This African violet is made up of two crowns.

Ferns are another example of plants that have to be divided. The matted root ball is pried apart and then cut into sections, each section containing a crown of leaves.

SINGLE-LEAF CUTTINGS

In water

If you have a favorite plant you would like to share with a friend, you can grow a single leaf in water, producing a new plant. This method can be used only for certain plants, particularly for African violets and begonias.

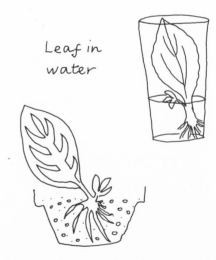

Leaf in water

Leaf in sand mixture

In sand or vermiculite

Many species of sedum and echeveria can be propagated from single-leaf cuttings. These are grown in sand or in vermiculite and form new plants at the base of the leaf.

12

FLAT-LEAF CUTTINGS

If you lay leaves of some plants on the soil, cut them through their veins, and give them bottom heat, new plantlets will form at the cuts. Begonia leaves can be treated this way as they are large and firm. The little plantlets that form can be lifted away from the mother plant gently and potted separately.

Back of leaf showing veins

Front of leaf

STEM CUTTINGS

A stem cutting is made from the main stem of an old plant that has lost most of its lower leaves. You can make a new plant by air layering or making a stem-tip cutting. First, cut off the topknot of the old plant; you are now left with a large expanse of scarred stem. This stem can be cut up into three-inch lengths, each piece containing an ''eye'' or ''bud,'' and laid horizontally, half-buried, in vermiculite. The new plant forms at the eye.

Cut three-inch pieces of stem.

Sorry-looking "palm tree"

This method is used for rooting old begonia rhizomes, dracaenas, dieffenbachias, Chinese evergreens and woody philodendron canes.

Stem cuttings require bottom heat, so this is an occasion when the yogurt maker is brought into service.

Stem half-buried in vermiculite

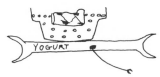

New shoot appears at eye.

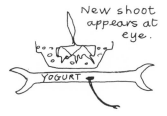

New shoot may appear below stub.

Don't throw away the old plant because sometimes a new shoot will appear on the stem just below the stub. Give it two months to form the shoot; if it doesn't appear by then, throw the plant away.

13

MALLET CUTTINGS

A stem cutting with a leaf attached is a mallet cutting. The stem is turned so that it lies horizontally on the vermiculite. Roots form at the node.

The new plant forms at the axil of the leaf, which is where the leaf joins the stem.

This method is used particularly when propagating big philodendrons.

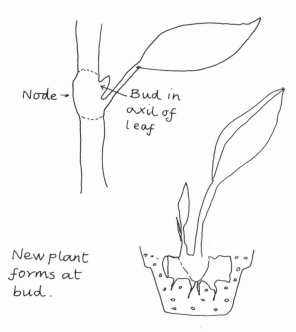

Node → Bud in axil of leaf

New plant forms at bud.

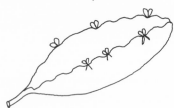

Kalanchoe pinnata

VIVIPAROUS PLANTS

These are plants that produce new plants rather than seeds. The popular piggyback plant is in this category. You can see the new plantlets forming on the tops of the large bottom leaves. These leaves will root in water only if the bottom leaf is submerged. The kalanchoes, which form new plantlets along the sides of their leaves, are also viviparous plants.

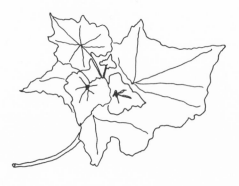

Piggyback leaf

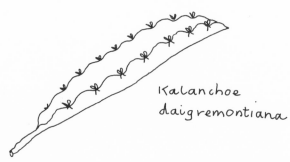

Kalanchoe daigremontiana

TUBERS AND CORMS

These are both loosely known as "bulbs," roots that carry their own life-support system around with them. They can be propagated during dormancy.

Tubers can be cut into pieces, each piece containing one "eye," as in a potato. A new plant grows from each piece. An example is the tuberous begonia.

Tuber cut into three pieces, each with an eye

Crocuses grow from little corms which form on top of the mother corm and are separated so that they will multiply.

Narcissus and daffodils grow from true bulbs. In the wild they propagate themselves by forming "bulbils," which are tiny bulbs. When grown in pots, however, they rarely bloom a second year, let alone propagate themselves.

Daffodil bulbs form bulbils.

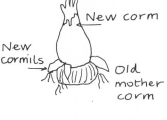

New corm

New cormils

Old mother corm

Crocus corm

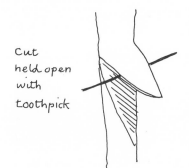

Cut held open with toothpick

AIR LAYERING

This method is used on the main stems of older plants that have lost their bottom leaves and have begun to look like palm trees.

Make a cut three-quarters of the way through the stem at an angle of 45 degrees. Insert a toothpick to keep the cut from sealing itself closed again. Wrap the cut in sphagnum moss which has been soaked in water and wrung out. Then wrap this in plastic and tie at the top and bottom with Twist-ems.

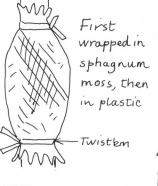

First wrapped in sphagnum moss, then in plastic

Twist'em

Roots grow through the moss.

Stem is cut below roots.

When roots appear through the moss, cut the stem just below the roots. Plant the whole root ball in a pot of soil. This method is used on older plants that grow from main stems and not from crowns. Examples are the rubber plant, the fiddle-leaf fig, schefflera and dracaena.

AFRICAN VIOLET

Gesneriad Family

(Saintpaulia ionantha)

I think that the secret to being an African-violet owner is that you must be prepared to devote your entire interest to them and them only. Real African-violet nuts have them on plant stands, cake stands, bookshelves, the dining-room table and practically everywhere else. They tend to their plants with such a single-minded dedication that their houses are always a mass of color.

I must admit that I am not that sort of person (even though I once grew a new African violet plant from a single leaf), so the following directions come to you via my friend Mildred, who is a real African-violet freak.

In spite of their being very fussy as adult plants, African violets are very easy to propagate. You can do this in several different ways: by removing offsets which form at the collar of the plant, by dividing the crowns, or by rooting a single leaf in water and removing the plantlets as they form.

Dividing the crowns

Most mature African-violet plants are made up of many crowns all sharing the same roots. They can be divided up into separate plants, each having a section of the roots.

Two separate crowns

Knock the plant out of its pot and, with your fingers, trace where the individual crowns emerge at the surface. Look closely and you will see how to pull these crowns gently away from one another. It should not be necessary to use a knife at all.

Each crown should be potted in a small pot of African-violet mix. This is an especially rich potting medium that is available at most plant shops.

16

Removing offsets

On a mature plant, you can see new crowns appearing at the base of the mother plant. These are called offsets. If the crown appears to be growing on top of the mother plant, it should be cut off and dusted with fungicide applied with a cotton swab. Prepare a two-inch pot with African-violet mix and press the offset gently into the mix.

If the offset appears to be growing from below the surface of the soil, it should be carefully cut away from the mother plant together with a small portion of her roots. The cut parts should be dusted with fungicide and planted in a pot filled with African-violet mix.

The plant may need to be propped up with toothpicks and will benefit from a few days in a greenhouse made from an upturned jam jar balanced on the rim of the pot.

Offset cut from mother plant

cut area

Propagating leaves

Creating a new plant from a single leaf is a marvelous exercise in plant propagation. The amazing thing about the African violet is that the same leaf can be used over and over again; each plantlet can be separated from the mother leaf as soon as its own roots are well formed.

Mature leaf with a two-inch stem

Plantlet

Plantlet goes into hole made for it in African-violet mix.

Some people poke the leaf through a paper or foil collar on a glass jar, but another way is to stand the leaf stalk in two inches of water at the bottom of a narrow drinking tumbler. The advantage of this method is that the leaf receives additional humidity from its proximity to the water.

Roots form from the cut end of the stalk, and small plantlets grow just above the roots. When the plantlets are one inch high, they can be carefully removed from the parent leaf with their own root system intact.

They should be potted in small two- to three-inch pots of African-violet mix, and the parent leaf can be left in the water to start producing again.

Using a cutting box

When you have a lot of leaves to propagate, you can use a cutting box such as a bread box made of transparent plastic with a fitted lid. Spread two inches of prepared vermiculite on the bottom. Then place the single leaves with their stems in a slanted position in the vermiculite, so that any moisture buildup will run off them and not cause them to rot.

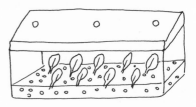

Cutting box filled with vermiculite

If the vermiculite is always kept moist and the humidity is kept up inside the cutting box, roots will form at the base of the stems and the plantlets will appear just above the vermiculite.

Leaf set sideways to give plantlet room

When the plantlets appear, the leaf should be taken out of the box and planted in a two-inch pot. Be sure to set the parent leaf sideways in the soil so that the new plantlet can get the light and have room to grow.

Bulb pot

Making a "cake-pan" pot

This is a useful pot to have when you have a lot of leaves to propagate. To make it, insert a two-inch clay pot into a wide, shallow bulb pot filled with vermiculite. Plug the bottom hole of the two-inch pot with chewing gum, and fill the pot with water. The trick to this pot is that the water in the small clay pot seeps through its sides into the vermiculite in the large pot, thus keeping it moist. The individual leaves are set in a slanted position in the vermiculite.

Two-inch pot

Roots form in the vermiculite, and the plantlets form at the base of the leaves just above the surface. As before, these plantlets should be potted separately.

chewing-gum stopper

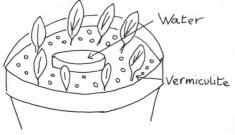

Water

Vermiculite

African-violet leaves root twice as fast if you place them in your brightest window, and they particularly benefit from a plant lamp. They like their soil moist but not wet, and Mildred uses only warm water—never cold—in watering them. (Didn't I tell you they're fussy?)

ALOE (Aloe) Lily Family

Aloes are the succulent members of the lily family, and the 200 species of aloe can be found in all sizes, from tiny to tree size. The aloes come from South Africa, where the seasons are the reverse of ours. You would think that over the years the aloes would have adjusted to the new cycle of seasons in this country, but they haven't. They still bloom during their summer, which is our winter, and their flowers are very welcome at a time when spring seems such a long way off.

Aloe variegata

Aloes have tender, fleshy leaves which grow in rosette form. Their leaves can be striped or spotted, smooth-edged or serrated with teeth. The *Aloe variegata* has a stiff central spine, making it appear almost three-sided. It is marked in bands of dark green, and its flowers, pink to red, appear on tall sprays. *A. striata* is called the "coral aloe" because its leaves have a pinkish edge.

A striata

A. vera

A. *vera* has sap that is used for treating burns. I once bought a bottle of it thinking that it was skin lotion. It wasn't until it was time to buy another bottle that I happened to glance at the label and read: "Take two teaspoons after meals." Which only goes to show that my dear eighty-year-old Dr. Fahey was right when he said: "Don't ever put anything on your skin that you wouldn't eat."

Aloes propagate by means of offsets which form at the base of the mother plant. They can be cut away with a sharp knife and put aside for a day or so to allow the cut area to form a scab. Because the leaves of the aloe act as a water reservoir, the offset will not wither and die while it is forming the scab.

offsets

Aloes like a dry soil, so you should mix up a soil recipe of half sand and half potting soil. Carefully press the offset into the soil, which should be moist but not wet or it will rot. Your little plant will appreciate the best light in the house.

APHELANDRA   Acanthus Family

(Aphelandra squarrosa louisae)

The aphelandra is sometimes called the "zebra plant" because of its green-and-white-striped leaves. It is that sensational plant your boss's wife sent you when you had your last baby. It was very expensive, so now you are feeling very guilty because it lost all its lower leaves as soon as you got it home.

Remove yellow spike of flower after blooming.

Well, what can you expect from a plant that started life in the jungles of Brazil and ended up on your mantelpiece? It loves the heat in your house but it must have humidity, whether this comes from twice-daily misting, setting it on pebbles in water, or taking it into the bathroom with you whenever you have a shower.

Tip cutting

So now you are left with a bare stem and a topknot of leaves. Make a tip cutting by removing the topknot with four inches of stem. Prepare a six-inch pot of vermiculite and use a stick to make a hole in the center, into which you put the stem. Water with a vitamin B_1 solution.

Cut here.

Provide humidity by putting the pot into a plastic bag or by covering it with a jam jar which has a bell wide enough that it doesn't touch the leaves. If too much moisture builds up, tear a few holes in the plastic bag or tilt the jam jar and place a small pebble on the rim of the pot. Roots will form in four to six weeks, and you can pot your plant in soil then.

Don't forget to "harden up" your plant. Over a period of five days tear larger and larger holes in the plastic bag until it is torn in half. Let more air into the jam jar each day by tilting it farther and farther.

As with all plants, the best time to make cuttings is in spring, but you don't have to wait until then if your plant is looking dreadfully bare in autumn. This method of tip cutting can be done over and over again. The new plant will last about nine months; it will bloom if you are lucky, but then lose all its lower leaves again. So you are right back where you started!

20

ASPARAGUS FERNS   Lily Family
(Asparagus sprengeri; A. plumosus; A. asparagoides myrtifolius)

Although we think of asparagus ferns as members of the fern family, they are actually the asparagus members of the lily family and not ferns at all.

Asparagus sprengeri, the most popular asparagus fern, is usually grown in hanging baskets because it trails so spectacularly. It is also moderately undemanding, which is always a relief. Its foliage is made up of tiny bright green needles, and it has clusters of white flowers which turn into red berries. These are the seeds, which, planted in small two-inch pots, will provide you new plants.

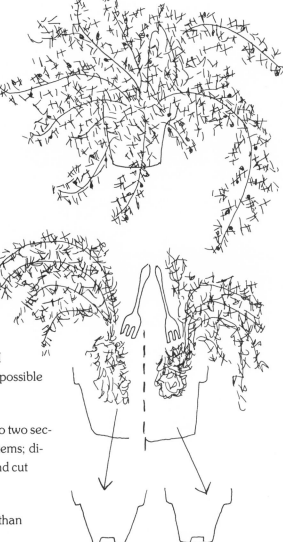

A. plumosus is that beautiful delicate fern that florists add to bouquets. It is an upright fern and can grow quite tall. It also produces small white flowers which become black berries and can be planted as seeds.

A. asparagoides myrtifolius is the "baby smilax" that florists use. It, too, has flowers that produce seeds which can be planted.

Division

Asparagus ferns are fast growers, and you will have to divide them often. All varieties can be divided in the same way.

Knock your plant out of its pot, and you will see the matted root ball with practically no soil left at all. I have often wondered what happens to the soil—is it possible that the roots *eat* it?

Take two strong forks and pull the matted roots into two sections. Make sure that one side doesn't have all the stems; divide them as evenly as possible. Take a sharp knife and cut the roots apart.

Each segment can be potted in a pot a little smaller than the one the original plant was in.

21

AVOCADO   *(Persea americana)*   Laurel Family

I always hesitate before throwing away the large pit of the avocado because there, in my hand, lies a potential tree. As a result, I have five avocado trees around the house in various stages of growth. Whether they come from Florida and have dark pebbly skins or from California and have smooth skins, they are propagated the same way.

When opening your avocado to eat it, be careful not to cut into the pit. Scoop it out of the fruit with a spoon and wash it off. Leave it aside overnight; by morning the papery skin will have cracked open and will peel off.

Rooting in water

It's far more fun growing an avocado in water because you can watch the root forming through the glass.

Dunce's cap covers pit until taproot appears.

Taproot

Find a glass or jar small enough to hold the pit in contact with the water without its falling through the opening. The flat bottom of the pit must be in contact with the water.

Many people mess around with toothpicks because they are too lazy to find a jar just the right size. However, if you have looked in vain, the toothpicks act as a prop to hold the pit at the right position in the water.

Toothpicks stuck in pit, balanced on lip of glass

Water

You can speed up the germinating process by making a "dunce's cap." Cut a circle of paper and fold it into four sections. Open up one of the sections, and you have a dunce's cap.

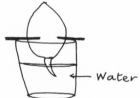

Cut a circle. Fold in half.

Fold in quarters.

Open up.

Shoot appears above root.

Although I have read that avocados need light to germinate, the pit with the dunce's cap produces its first root in two weeks in contrast to the more usual time of two months. Once the thick root appears at the base of the pit, you can remove the cap.

As your avocado is about to produce its first shoot, it will give the appearance of splitting apart and the shoot will appear directly above the root from the center of the pit. As soon as there are two pairs of leaves, you can pot the avocado in potting soil.

Potting

Take a six-inch pot, crock it and half fill it with potting soil. Make a hole in the center of the pot deep enough to take the pit and its root. Add enough soil to cover the pit and leave the stem and leaves above the surface. Water with a vitamin B_1 solution.

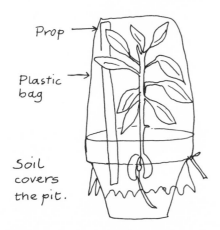

Prop

Plastic bag

Soil covers the pit.

This transfer from water to soil is always a shock for a young plant, so I would advise you to pop it into a plastic bag immediately for the greenhouse treatment. This will allow the young leaves to absorb moisture while the roots are adjusting to the soil.

Prop up the bag with chopsticks so that it won't fall on the young leaves. After a few days, if there is no sign of wilting you can harden up your plant by opening the plastic bag a little at a time.

Pruning

Once your little tree is six inches tall, it is time to think of pruning. What is known as pinching back in plants is called pruning in trees.

Taking off a couple of inches from the top may seem unnecessarily brutal, but this encourages branching further down, creating a better shaped tree.

A good rule to follow when pruning a tree is to never cut back more than one-third of its height. This applies whether the tree is six inches or six feet tall.

As your tree matures, remember to repot it each year. Always choose a pot a few inches larger than the last one. Don't jump from a small pot to a large one.

Even though you fertilize your avocado tree monthly, it is most unlikely that it will ever produce fruit. This does not mean that you haven't taken good enough care of it; it's just that your living room probably can't provide the right environment for a tree that is used to growing outside in a field. However, as the avocado tree is a beautiful and graceful tree whether it produces fruit or not, be proud that you created it (with a little help from Mother Nature) all by yourself.

BEGONIA　　　　*(Begonia)*　　　Begonia Family

Begonias as a group are important enough to have their own family name. They are grouped according to their root type: tuberous, fibrous and rhizomatous. Tuberous begonias are loveliest of all but, alas, they won't grow indoors. They are those glorious pastel-colored begonias that hang out of their baskets like chiffon party dresses.

FIBROUS BEGONIAS

BEGONIA ELATIOR AND *B. SEMPERFLORENS*

Begonia elatior is almost as pretty as the tuberous begonia but has the advantage of doing very well indoors. The *B. semperflorens* (meaning "everflowering"), is the pretty little begonia with the shiny roundish leaves and pink, white, or red flowers the size of a penny. It blooms on and off all year, hence its name. Its leaves, green in winter, will turn red in the summer if you put it outdoors in the sun.

Begonia elatior

B. semperflorens

The secret to keeping all fibrous-rooted begonias in good shape is to cut them back whenever they begin to look scraggly. This leaves you with a bunch of stem cuttings.

Because their stems are fragile and inclined to snap, you should use the "two-stage" pot so that you won't have to repot them again at a later stage. To make it, put a peat pot filled with vermiculite into a larger bulb pot filled with potting soil. The cuttings form roots in the vermiculite and will eventually grow through the sides of the peat pot into the potting soil.

Put the pot into a plastic-bag greenhouse propped up with a chopstick to hold the plastic away from the leaves. Place on the yogurt maker for bottom heat.

These cuttings need good bright light to form roots. After one month, remove from the yogurt maker and harden up your new plant by opening up the plastic bag slowly.

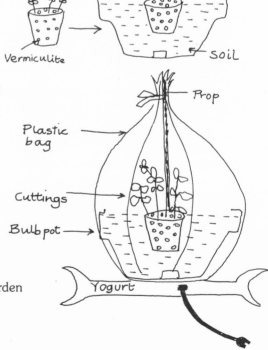

Peat pot goes into bulb pot.

Vermiculite

Soil

Prop

Plastic bag

Cuttings

Bulb pot

Yogurt

ANGEL-WING BEGONIAS

Angel-wing begonias are fibrous-rooted begonias with a cane stem. These are large begonias and are so named because of their lopsided leaves shaped like angels' wings. They have thicker stems than *B. semperflorens* and are not so fragile.

To propagate an angel-wing, take a tip cutting of four or five inches and root it in water or vermiculite.

When rooting in water, you must take extra precautions against wilting when potting the cutting in soil because of the very fine roots that form. Give it vitamin B_1 to ward off shock and put it into a plastic-bag greenhouse for a week. If the stem and leaves are firm and crisp, you can gradually harden it up.

When rooting in vermiculite, the stem will stay upright without a prop. Roots will form in four to six weeks, and the cutting can then be potted in soil.

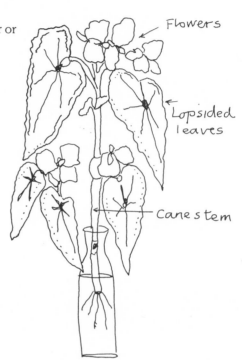

Flowers

Lopsided leaves

Cane stem

Pink sprays

Lettuce-type leaves

Rhizome

RHIZOMATOUS BEGONIAS

These begonias grow from a scarred rhizome, which is a thick fleshy stem that grows above the surface but sends down roots into the soil. The rhizome stores water in its thick stem, so you must be careful not to overwater it or it will rot.

I got my cutting from my neighbor Polly, who had a beautiful plant that I had been eyeing for some time. We didn't know its name, so we looked it up in *Exotica*, a pictorial cyclopedia of exotic plants. There, among the 1,200 varieties of begonia, we found it: *B.* 'Ricky Minter.' So thank you, Mr. Minter. We love your begonia. It has dark green ruffled leaves, which are quite large, and in the spring it sends up beautiful lacy sprays of pink flowers.

Stem cutting

As one of the rhizomes had lost most of its lower leaves, I decided to propagate it by cutting off a piece of the stem with its topknot of leaves.

I crocked a shallow pot and filled it with half potting soil and half sand in order to provide good drainage. I half-buried the stem horizontally in the soil and put the pot into a plastic-bag greenhouse.

The cutting began to wilt in a horrible fashion, and this is when I got the idea of using the yogurt maker to provide bottom heat. It was a fortunate idea, as the cutting recovered within twenty-four hours. I kept it on the yogurt maker for a month and then let it harden up very slowly. It is doing very well, and this spring it put out its first flowers.

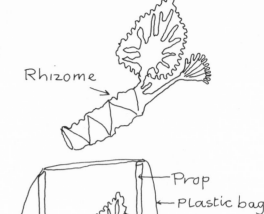

Rhizome

Prop

Plastic bag

Half-buried in sand mixture

BEST YOGURT

REX BEGONIAS

Rex begonias are grown chiefly for their beautiful leaves, which are large and firm. A method used to propagate them is "leaf propagation," by which one leaf can be forced to put out many tiny plants. This is a very slow method of propagation, but it is rewarding to do.

Cuts at veins

Take a mature leaf from your plant and turn it over. You will see the main veins running from the central stem. Take a very sharp knife and make cuts across these veins.

Leaf lies flat on soil mix.

Plastic wrap
string

YOGURT

Now turn the leaf face upward and lay it on the surface of a shallow pot filled with half soil and half sand. Make sure that the stem is pushed into the soil, as this will prevent it from popping up. Put little pebbles onto the leaf to hold it in contact with the soil.

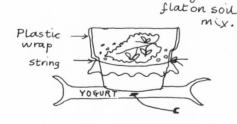

New plantlet ready to be potted

Cover the pot with plastic wrap and place it on the yogurt maker. New plantlets will form at the cuts; when they have two pairs of leaves, you can transplant them very carefully to small pots of their own. Don't forget to harden up your plants before removing them from their plastic greenhouse. (See page 8.)

26

BIRD'S-NEST FERN   *(Asplenium nidus)*   Fern Family

This very popular fern looks more like a bromeliad than a fern, as it grows from a central rosette and its leaves are not divided like fern fronds. This is a charming plant when it is young with its rippled pale green leaves, but it can grow to three feet tall and get a little ungainly.

Asplenium nidus propagates itself by putting out offsets at its base which can be removed with a sharp knife. As with all offsets, it is wise to try to cut off a piece of the mother plant's roots when you are removing the offset, since this gives the baby a head start.

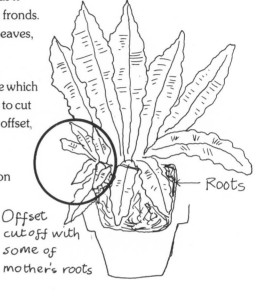

Roots

Knock the plant out of its pot and trace the offset's root formation down to where it joins its mother. Cut it there. Plant it in a pot of prepared vermiculite deep enough to hold the roots without squashing them. Cover the pot with a jam jar and set it on the yogurt maker, as it will do far better with bottom heat.

Offset cut off with some of mother's roots

Tilt

In two weeks your plant's new roots will have adjusted to feeding the young offset and you can take it off the heat. Harden up your plant by raising the jam jar slowly. Repot the new plant in potting soil in the same size pot.

"MOTHER SPLEENWORT" *(Asplenium bulbiferum)*

This fern is viviparous; that is, it produces new plantlets on its leaves rather than producing seeds. This is a very delicate fern, looking a little like a carrot top. The offspring grow along the edges of the leaf, and you really need a magnifying glass to see them.

Keep up water level.

To propagate, break up a frond into sections and lay it flat in water. Each tiny plant will form roots and in a few weeks can be put into a small pot of soil. You will help the growing process by using a plant light.

Add some leaf mold to the potting soil; it grows best in a porous soil which should never be allowed to dry out.

27

BOSTON FERN   Fern Family
(Nephrolepis exaltata bostoniensis)

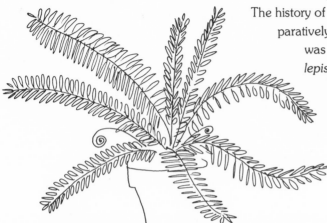

Nephrolepis exaltata bostoniensis

The history of the Boston fern is interesting because it is a comparatively recent mutation of the common sword fern. It was discovered quite by chance in a batch of *Nephrolepis exaltata* in the late nineteenth century. The shipper noticed that one of the plants had broader leaves and was generally larger and more graceful than the rest of the shipment. He separated it from the others, and from this one plant come the hundreds of thousands of Boston ferns that decorate our houses.

And it continues to evolve—almost every year new and more fantastic varieties of *N. exaltata* come onto the market. I counted forty-one, and I am sure there are more to come. Of these perhaps *N. exaltata whitmanii* is the most beautiful—or is it *N. exaltata* 'Fluffy Ruffles'? They are all so gorgeous, how can anyone choose?

As with all members of the fern family, you have to try to adapt your living room to suit them. Although their natural habitat was the floors of sun-dappled forests, they need good light to prosper indoors and even benefit from a plant light.

And they need humidity; otherwise, those telltale burned ends will start ruining their appearance. Mist them daily and, if possible, take them into the bathroom with you once a week and after you have showered, put them into the shower stall and close the door. Another method is to put them into the bathroom, close the windows and door, and run the hot water. (In fact, this is the same thing you do to get creases out of clothes.) This treatment works wonders on all my ferns.

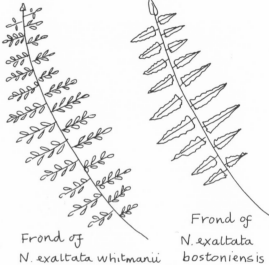

Frond of
N. exaltata whitmanii

Frond of
N. exaltata bostoniensis

Ferns love steam.

28

Boston ferns need to be well watered, and they often become root-bound because they grow very fast. When the water comes straight out of the bottom hole onto your shoes, your plant is root-bound. Using ice cubes with their slow rate of melting takes care of the problem for the moment, but sooner or later you must either transplant your fern to a larger pot or divide it.

Division

Knock the plant out of its pot, and you can see that the matted roots look like a bird's nest. Around the edge of the pot are small runners, offsets with tiny fronds uncurling on them. Cut these off separately, taking some of the roots with them. Pot each tiny offset in a separate pot. They will eventually become large plants—in about five years.

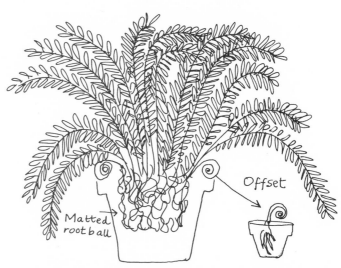

One large fern made up of three separate crowns

What you originally thought of as one fern is really made up of many smaller crowns. If you look closely, you can see where each separate crown grows up from the roots. Take two forks and try to pull the crowns apart, separating the roots. It is hard work, and many people give up at this stage and take a hatchet to cut the plant in two. This doesn't kill your plant, but I don't think that it is particularly good for it either.

When you have a general idea as to how the roots and crowns can be separated, take a sharp knife and make the division. Each clump of roots must have one or two crowns of leaves.

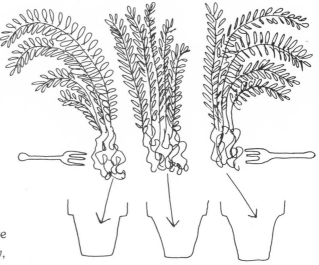

Crock three- or four-inch pots and plant each crown in its own pot. If you prefer, you can plant two or three crowns together to give a fuller effect. Boston ferns grow very quickly, and you may find that a year later you have to repot your plant in a much larger pot. Then each year after that a larger and larger pot will be needed, until it is time to divide the plant again. It's hardest to do the first time, but you will feel more confident the next time you divide your plant. You see, I was right! Confidence *does* come with experience.

BROMELIAD   Pineapple Family
(Aechmea; Billbergia; Guzmania; Vriesia)

Don't do what I did and go out and try to buy a bromeliad tree—they laughed at me in the plant shop and it was all very embarrassing. But I had seen a photograph of a bromeliad tree and wanted one just like it. What I hadn't realized was that the "tree" was in fact formed by taking some old dead branches and planting bromeliads at auspicious points.

Bromeliad tree

Bromeliads are epiphytic, which means that they grow in the air rather than on the floor of their native habitat, the South American jungle. Their roots merely act as anchors hooking them to the trunks of trees, while their leaves absorb nutrients from the rain and dew, this moisture being stored in the natural vase formed at the base of the leaves.

Aechmea fasciata 'Silver King'

Aechmeas are cousins of the pineapple and the most popular form of bromeliad. A lovely member of the aechmeas is *Aechmea fasciata* 'Silver King,' which has silvery leaves in rosette form and a silver-pink flower. Other favorites are: *A. purpurea,* with purple bands on the leaves and pink and blue flowers, and *A.* 'Foster's Favorite' (named, I hope, after Mrs. Foster), with spikes of dark blue flowers.

Cryptanthus, cousins of the aechmeas, are known as earth stars. They have striped leaves of green and silver. These are lovely plants to own because their flowers last a long time and are so gloriously beautiful to look at. The plants need to be misted with water regularly, and twice a month they should be sprayed with a weak solution of fertilizer, as they feed through their leaves. Their growing medium should be kept moist.

Other popular bromeliads are tillandsia, vriesia, guzmania, neoregelia and billbergia.

A. 'Foster's Favorite'

A. Cryptanthus

Bromeliads propagate themselves through offsets which form at the base of the mother plant. Each mother has a one-year life span but produces many children to carry on the family name.

It is possible to cut off these offsets with a sharp knife, but be sure to leave at least one behind, because next year that one will become the new mother plant at the old homestead.

Building a bromeliad tree

You must have the following: bromeliad offsets, a piece of driftwood, various growing mediums and fine picture wire.

If you live near an orchid nursery, you can buy the growing medium already prepared, which will save a lot of trouble. If not, it will be necessary to make it yourself.

You will need the following: coarse leaf mold made from decomposed leaves; shredded bark, which is tree bark broken up into small pieces; peat moss, which is decomposed sphagnum moss; and osmunda fiber, which is made from the dried roots of the osmunda fern and will be used to hold the other ingredients together in a kind of "cup." All these things should be available at exotic plant shops. If the osmunda fiber is unobtainable, sphagnum moss may be substituted.

Soak the osmunda fiber in water and wring it out. Lay it flat. Take a handful of the growing medium and lay it in the center of the osmunda fiber. Place your bromeliad offset in the center of the growing medium. Now wrap the osmunda fiber around the offset and the soil, forming a kind of "cup."

Take the picture wire and wrap it firmly around the cup. Now secure the cup to the driftwood with picture wire. It will look very bottom heavy at first; but as the plant grows, its leaves will hang down and hide the fiber base. If you repeat this process four times, you will end up with a bromeliad tree.

Offsets form at base.

Secured to the tree with fine picture wire

CACTI   *(Epiphyllum; Opuntia; Schlumbergera)*   Cactus Family

Cactus plants make charming houseguests and will even flower for you if you grow them under plant lights. They are the easiest plants in the world to propagate because you can take cuttings and offsets from them, and they will grow in sandy soil. All cacti need to form a callus after they are cut, so you must leave them aside for a day or two before planting in soil.

The most familiar cactus is the prickly-pear *(Opuntia macrodasys).* Any of the "ears" can be cut off to form a new plant. After it has formed a callus, make up a soil mixture consisting of three-quarters sand and one-quarter soil.

Opuntia

The beloved Christmas cactus *(Schlumbergera bridgesii)* grows best in a slightly denser soil, so make it up with half potting soil and half sand. This lovely cactus is formed of "joints" that grow on top of one another. Cut off one of these joints, let it form a callus, then root it in the sandy soil and you will have a new plant.

Christmas cactus

offsets

This cactus will bloom for you if you put it into the same cupboard as the poinsettia (see page 80); it is a light-sensitive plant that needs long, dark nights in autumn to form flowers at Christmas.

Red flower

Because most cacti come from desert regions, they require bright light and good drainage. Even the cuttings require very little water —wet the sandy soil when you first plant them and let the sand dry out completely before adding any more water. Although cacti have interesting shapes, it is their flowers that make them so unique—when they flower it is like being presented with a wonderful gift.

My neighbor has many cacti in his garden, including an epiphyllum which bloomed this year while he was away. I marked the date down for him, and he is making a point of arranging his calendar for next year so that he won't miss the beautiful flowers.

Epiphyllum 'ackermannii'

CALADIUM

Arum or Calla Family

(Caladium bicolor)

Caladiums are those beautiful plants with the paper-thin elephant-ear leaves that seem almost transparent and are splashed with all the colors of the rainbow.

Caladium candidum

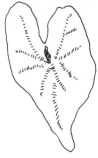

'Jessie Thayer'

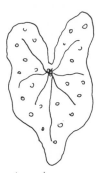

'Twinkles'

'Itacapus'

Caladiums are grown from tubers and, like all tuberous plants, they have a growing season and a resting season. During the growing season when the plant is putting out new leaves, it should be watered liberally. When the leaves appear to be fading and no new growth is visible, you should gradually cut down the amount of water you give it and the number of times you water it.

Remnants of the bloom can be cut off and the plant can be taken from its window position and put somewhere out of the way while it rests. To keep the tuber from drying out completely, give it one cupful of water every two weeks, pouring the water around the sides of the pot rather than on the tuber. After the plant rests for two months, you will notice that small leaves are beginning to appear. This is an indication that your plant is ready to wake up.

Caladium tuber, cut into three pieces

Caladium tubers, like the potato, can be cut up into many pieces, each piece containing an "eye" which will become a new plant.

Dividing the tuber

Remove your tuber from its pot and carefully look it over to see where its eyes are. Cut it so that each section has an eye. Dust each piece with a hormone-rooting powder that contains a fungicide.

Prepare a seed box or a large bulb pot with chopped-up sphagnum moss and water it well. Cover the tuber sections to a depth of one inch. The moss must be kept moist and the temperature should be high, from 75 to 85 degrees Fahrenheit. If your home is not this warm, set the box or pot on the yogurt maker.

Keep checking the tubers until you can see that new roots have formed. Each section should be planted in potting soil in a small pot. At this stage tubers like to be pot-bound, so use a three-inch pot.

As they grow bigger, you can use a larger size pot. They do best with bright light and benefit enormously from plant lights.

In bulb pot on yogurt maker

Plastic wrap

New shoots appear after roots have formed.

Soil

Ready for potting in a three-inch pot

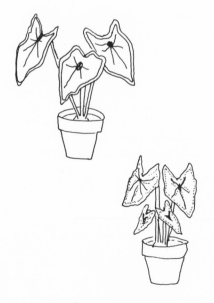

Caladiums are plants that look wonderful in the plant shop but are disappointing when you get them home. This is because one on its own gets lost. When you make your original purchase, if you can afford it get two smaller plants instead of one large one. The next year you will benefit from lots of baby caladiums and be able to put on a good show.

Fertilize them every two weeks during their growing period but not at all while they are dormant.

CHINESE EVERGREEN
Arum or Calla Family
(Aglaonema modestum)

Aglaonema modestum, commonly known as Chinese evergreen, is a popular houseplant with good reason—it has beautiful green leaves, often with silver markings, and a spathe-type flower like a small lily. Its dark green leaves indicate that it does not require bright light. However, I found that as soon as I set it on a windowsill, it perked up immediately and produced a flower.

As young plants, the stems appear to grow directly out of the soil; but as they grow taller, you can see that the stems are attached to a thick canelike "trunk." The lower leaves have the habit of turning yellow and dropping off, so you will be left with a long scarred stem and a topknot of leaves.

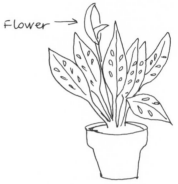

Young plant

Flower →

Older plant

Thick stem

Flower produces seeds.

Offsets

Tiny offset

Topknot of leaves with three inches of stem

This plant will often put out offsets, tiny plants at the soil level. These can be removed with a sharp knife and will form roots in water.

However, if your plant is growing taller and taller and you have removed any offsets that might otherwise camouflage the bare stem, you have to be prepared for extreme action. Cut off the topknot of leaves with three inches of stem. This will form roots easily in water; in fact, many people never bother to pot it in soil as it grows so well in water.

Stem Propagation

You are now left with a very ugly stub and a long scarred stem. Cut the stem into three-inch pieces.

Crock a shallow pot and fill it with a mixture of half sand and half potting soil. Lay the pieces of stem on top of the soil and press them into it until they are half-buried.

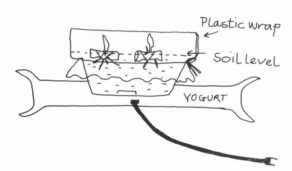

Three-inch pieces

Plastic wrap

Soil level

YOGURT

Cover the pot with plastic wrap tied with string under the lip of the pot. Set it on the yogurt maker.

Stem propagation is difficult to accomplish because sometimes the old stem has completely forgotten how to do it. But with bottom heat and a greenhouse you have a very good chance of jogging your old stem into activity.

You are left with a one-inch stub sitting in the pot. Don't throw it away yet because there is still a chance that it might put out one or even two shoots on either side of the stub.

Put it somewhere where it won't be the object of attention and wait a month or two to see if anything happens. If it is quite obvious that, in spite of watering and watching over, your plant has departed for better fields, throw it away and wash out the pot—but not until then.

A new shoot! And I thought my life was finished.

Beheading a plant in this manner requires a lot of confidence. Think to yourself that you are creating new growth, not mutilating your plant. In the same manner that doctors only reset broken limbs, leaving nature to do the healing, you are only providing the right atmosphere for the plant, leaving Mother Nature to do the growing. And out of one old and battered plant you are making two or three new ones.

COLEUS   *(Coleus blumei)*   Mint Family

You must treat this plant very sternly, pinching it back constantly, to prevent it from growing spindly and looking like a weed (which isn't far from the truth, as its relatives are the common nettles). Under bright lights coleus is a beautifully colored plant, but it becomes less and less interesting as light diminishes. Coleus is found in a rainbowlike assortment of colors and leaf shapes. One of the most popular is *Coleus blumei*, which has serrated leaves and brightly colored centers. Like its cousin creeping Charlie, it throws up spikes of flowers, but most people remove them from coleus because they are not very pretty and detract from the beauty of the leaves.

Coleus blumei 'Brilliancy'

C. blumei 'Pyrenees Gold'

C. blumei 'Firebrand'

C. blumei 'Frilled Fantasy'

Rooting

Coleus must be the rabbit of the plant kingdom, as it will root in water in twenty-four hours flat—and I even read that under a plant light a cutting rooted in one hour! Thus, this is a very good plant for beginners, since it requires constant pruning to keep it in good shape and you can root each cutting.

Coleus is one of those rare plants that I recommend rooting directly in soil, bypassing the vermiculite stage.

By taking a lot of tip cuttings and planting them directly in the soil, you have an instant plant.

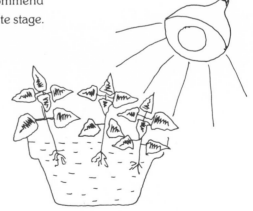

The tip cuttings should have at least two pairs of leaves. The soil must be kept moist, and the cuttings have to be in bright light. If you are not sure if your windowsill is bright enough, put the pot under a plant light if you have one.

I always think of coleus as a "disposable plant"—the original plant always gets very ungainly looking after a year or so, but the cuttings go on and on, providing new plants ad infinitum. So I usually dispose of the mother plant after a while and concentrate on her children.

37

CREEPING CHARLIE *(Plectranthus australis)* Mint Family

In California plectranthus is commonly called "creeping Charlie," but it seems that everywhere else it is known as "Swedish ivy." How the Swedes ever got into the act, I will never know because the plant originally came from Australia! No matter what its real name, it is a marvelous plant, beloved by all and a prodigious grower under the right conditions, which are bright light and careful watering.

My balcony

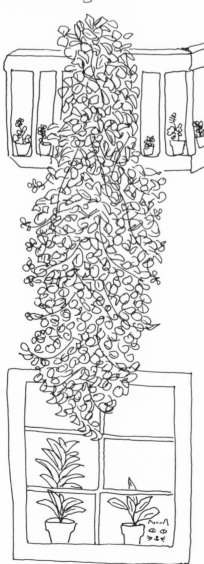

Charlie needs your brightest window plus some sunshine. If you have any doubts as to whether it is getting enough light, supplement it with a plant light. For the second condition, water, you must learn to recognize an "overwatered" droop from an "underwatered" droop. The first is fatal, but the second is reversible.

I once gave a nice young Charlie to a friend for her new shop. I cautioned her to place it in the window, but she preferred the aesthetic effect created by hanging it in the middle of the room. Of course the poor plant grew limp and gray-looking, and everyone advised her to give it more water. R.I.P.

A healthy Charlie has stiff stems and shiny leaves. The secret to watering Charlie is to use ice cubes. As your plant grows bigger and bigger, its roots take up more and more space until they pull the soil away from the sides of the pot. Then when you water it, the water runs straight down the sides and out of the bottom. When you use ice cubes, they dissolve so slowly that you can be sure the roots are getting as much water as they need.

Creeping Charlie is such a fast grower that you will need to take tip cuttings all the time, if only to keep the plant under control. I had one that got away from me, and in desperation I set it on the upstairs balcony. At last count it was over ten feet long and beginning to block the light coming through the downstairs window.

"Two-stage" pot

In spite of its enthusiastic growing habits, Charlie is quite a fragile plant and its brittle stems snap very easily when it is moved around. The "two-stage" pot is ideal for rooting Charlie cuttings. This pot was thought up by my editor and is a very clever solution to the problem of rooting fragile-stemmed cuttings that always break on transfer to soil.

Cutting

Fill a small peat pot with vermiculite and insert it into the large bulb pot filled with potting soil. The cuttings root in the vermiculite and work their way through the sides of the peat pot (which eventually disintegrates) and into the soil.

Peat pot inserted into bulb pot

Vermiculite *Potting soil*

Rooting cuttings in water

Charlie cuttings grow very well in water for a month or two, but then they lose their bottom leaves and die. So once the fine roots are well formed, you should transfer them to soil.

If you have six pieces growing together in a bottle, take them out without trying to separate their fine roots, as they will break. Crock a pot and fill it with potting soil. Make a hole in the center of the soil and put the rooted stems into the hole. Press the soil carefully around the stems and water well.

Roots form in water.

Plants transferred from water to soil invariably wilt and take a while to recover from the shock. Give them an antishock treatment by watering with a vitamin B_1 solution for a week. A few days in a plastic-bag greenhouse will also help them recover from the transfer.

Transferred to soil

Don't forget to pinch back your Charlie by taking tip cuttings as often as possible, because the more cuttings you take, the bushier your plant will be. It pays to be greedy!

CROTON   *(Codiaeum variegatum pictum)*   Spurge Family

If you have been wondering what you did wrong that caused your lovely croton to lose all its bottom leaves, join the club!

The secret to keeping a croton happy is to give it warmth and humidity, and good light with some sunshine, but not too much. In other words, it is very fussy. It needs bright light to bring out the color of its leaves, but if it gets too much, they will burn. And the colors of the leaves! They represent all the colors of the rainbow, from green through orange, red, pink, yellow and purple.

This plant is the despair of amateurs everywhere because it is so perfect when you first get it; but gradually it loses its leaves, and you are left with a stalk denuded of foliage but with a topknot. In a small plant you can make a tip cutting. In a large plant you can air layer the stems with good results.

Codiaeum variegatum 'Mons. Florin'

C. variegatum 'Irene Kingsley'

Tip cuttings

With a sharp knife, sever the stem four inches below the bottom leaf. Put it into a small pot of prepared vermiculite. It will root faster with bottom heat, so set it on the yogurt maker. Cover the cutting with a jam jar balanced on the lip of the flowerpot. Water it with a solution of vitamin B_1, which acts as a root stimulant and an antishock treatment.

It should remain in its greenhouse on the yogurt maker for a month. Remove it from the heat before hardening up. Tilt the jar a little more each day for five days. Once the plant has hardened up, repot it in potting soil.

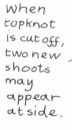

When topknot is cut off, two new shoots may appear at side.

Yogurt

Air Layering

Remember that new roots will grow from the place where the stem is cut, so it is better to have too little stem than too much.

Make a cut three-quarters of the way through the stem at an angle of 45 degrees. Insert a toothpick into the cut to keep it from sealing itself shut again.

New roots will grow at the cut.

Toothpick

40

Wrap the cut in sphagnum moss which has been soaked in water and wrung out. Cover the bundle of sphagnum moss in plastic wrap and tie it at the top and bottom with Twist-ems. A mist should form on the inside of the plastic wrap. If no mist is visible, unwind the top Twist-em and add a little water, dripping it onto the moss with a meat baster.

When roots appear through the moss, cut off the stem just below the roots. Remove the plastic wrap and plant the whole root ball in a pot of soil.

Don't throw away the original plant because sometimes it obligingly puts out a new shoot just below the stub. Continue watering it and let's hope that you will be lucky.

Crotons are a little like African violets—you have to be prepared to devote your life to them or they won't flourish. When I lived in London, I was a short distance away from a lovely old lady who had a greenhouse attached to her kitchen. It was a very nice setup, as she could keep her plants company while she was cooking. One day I arrived unexpectedly and, when no one answered the bell, I pushed the door open and walked in. There was no sign of my friend, but I could hear a monotonous humming sound coming from the kitchen. I went in to see if the kettle was whistling. However, I discovered that the sound I could hear was my friend serenading her plants (and this was long before it was the fashionable thing to do). She behaved as if it were the most natural thing in the world to do, so I didn't say anything.

In later years I have tried to do a bit of serenading myself, anxious to see whether my plants would grow toward (or away from) the sound. I don't know whether the plants enjoy it, but all I can say is that at the first peep from me, Whiskers, my old yellow cat, lumbers slowly out of his chair, walks to the front door, and pointedly *demands* to be let out.

It is really most humiliating, but I suppose that I am very lucky that none of my plants have feet.

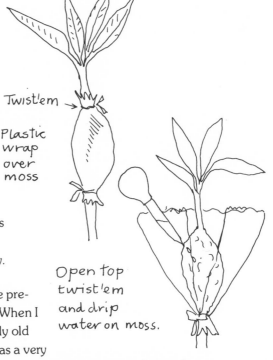

Twist'em →

Plastic
wrap
over
moss

Open top
twist'em
and drip
water on moss.

Land of ho-pe and Glo-ry . . .

CYCLAMEN *(Cyclamen)* Primrose Family

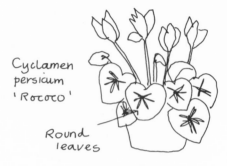

Cyclamen persicum 'Rococo'

Round leaves

The cyclamen, primrose and primula are all members of the same family. But whereas the primrose will grow wild in the country, covering the floor of the forest with beautiful yellow flowers, I have never seen a cyclamen that didn't come straight from the florist in a pot.

Heart-shaped leaves →

C. persicum 'Mary Perkins'

You are most definitely going to be given a cyclamen at some time in your life. It will flower most beautifully, and then it will look as if it is dying of starvation; gradually it will wither away and when it resembles an old boot, you will throw it out.

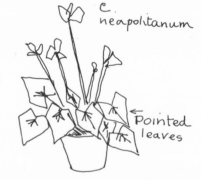

C. neapolitanum

← Pointed leaves

But wait—there is something you can do. Cyclamens grow from tubers, and tubers need to hibernate in the winter. So with this in mind, don't throw away your plant once it has "died." It is only preparing itself for its second coming.

Old pot   New pot

Same level

Take it out of its nasty plastic pot and repot it in a slightly larger clay pot. Keep the tuber at the same level in the new pot; in other words, if it was sticking out of the soil, in its original pot, replant it sticking out of the soil and not at the bottom of the new pot covered with four inches of soil.

Cut off any withered flowers and leaves and put it aside, almost forgetting that you have it. Give it a cupful of water every two weeks. Pour the water around the sides of the pot and not directly on the tuber.

After approximately two months, new growth will start appearing. Put the pot back into the light and commence watering regularly. A secret to having a cyclamen that flowers almost all the year round is to grow it under a plant light.

DATES

(Phoenix dactylifera)

Palm Family

If you buy your food from health-food stores, you are probably familiar with their wonderful dried dates, which seem to taste quite different from the usual boxed supermarket variety. They taste fresher because they are unsulfured and, thus unprotected from bugs and bacteria, can't be left on the shelves for months without spoiling. Being unsulfured has an additional advantage to us because their pits are capable of germinating—something their supermarket relatives cannot do.

Take a shallow glass or plastic container with a tight-fitting lid and line the bottom of it with surgical gauze, cut four or five layers thick. Wet the gauze thoroughly and drain off any surplus water. Put in your washed date pits, cover the container and put it into a brown paper bag in a dark place. If your container is tightly closed, you may not have to add any water until germination has taken place; but as this can take up to three months to happen, you had better check it out every few days.

Germinating container

Gauze →

When germination occurs, you will see a white root appear, similar to that in an avocado pit; this is the taproot. It will bury itself deep in the ground, so get a six-inch pot, crock it and fill it with a mixture of half sand and half potting soil. Make a hole for the taproot to go into and lay the pit horizontally over the hole. Cover it with soil.

Wait patiently.

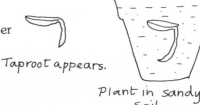

Taproot appears.

Plant in sandy soil.

The taproot will do most of the growing at first, so you won't see anything occurring above the surface. Eventually a small shoot will appear above the soil, and this is your new date palm.

Remember that these palms are desert growers and benefit from excellent light and moderate amounts of water. Let the topsoil get dry before rewatering. Will you get dates? Well, don't count on it. Just enjoy your pretty palm and be proud that you germinated it yourself.

New palm tree

DEVIL'S IVY *(Scindapsus aureus)* Arum or Calla Family

This plant has so many names that it can get confusing. I always thought that it was a variegated philodendron because its leaves are almost identical in shape to the *Philodendron cordatum.* But it is from a different family altogether and is called scindapsus or pothos. Its leaves are variegated, either flecked with yellow or silver, and the most popular variety is 'Marble Queen.' Devil's ivy can grow to enormous sizes with leathery leaves and aerial roots that hang down. The leaves of a mature plant can be two feet long with perforations like monstera.

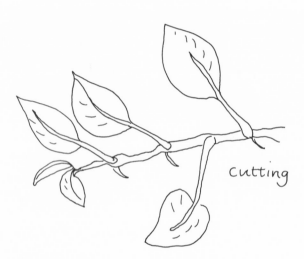

cutting

When buying a new plant, look for one with several stems at soil level rather than with one or two long trailing stems.

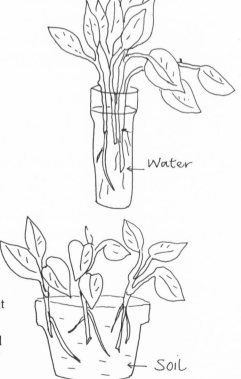

Water

Soil

Tip cuttings

The easiest way to grow a new plant is from tip cuttings. Break off four-inch pieces of stem and root them in water. The roots form very quickly. If you like the looks of roots growing in water, you can leave them there forever, as they seem to get all the nourishment they need from the water.

If you want to put them into a pot, crock the pot and fill it with potting soil. Take four or five rooted cuttings and put each piece into a hole made for it with a stick. Press the soil carefully around the stems. Water it well, and you have an instant plant.

Sometimes your plant will have one or two long trailing stems, and it will look very bare at the soil level. In this case wind the stems around the inner lip of the pot and pin them down with long hairpins. Place the hairpins at the nodes of the stem and make sure that you bruise the stem a little as you insert the hairpin. This bruising will cause the stem to form a self-protective callus, and new roots will form at this spot.

Trailing stem

Hairpins

This is an exceptional plant to use in a mixed planting. It will happily share its pot with a spider plant and some grape ivy. They all have approximately the same light and water requirements, and they look well together.

Watering

Devil's ivy has a useful way of letting you know when it needs watering. It will go limp and flop in its pot. After watering, you will notice that it stiffens up and looks like its old shiny, healthy self again.

Unfortunately, however, devil's ivy also droops and flops when it has been overwatered, so you must learn to recognize an "overwatered droop" from an "underwatered droop." If your plant is limp and you watered it only yesterday, the first thing to do is to pick up the pot and see if it feels light or heavy. If it is heavy, you must spring into action. Try knocking the plant out of its pot and completely repotting it with new soil. Alternatively, you could set the pot on the yogurt maker without covering it with a plastic bag. This will cause the soil to dry out.

The easiest way to know if your plant is wet or dry is to buy one of those gadgets that tell you. Some of these have an arrow that points and are very reliable. I had an excellent one that worked perfectly until it was used to pry open a jam jar. Somehow it never seemed to work properly after that. At present I have one that buzzes fast when wet and slow when dry; and whenever I am in doubt, I use it. At least I can be sure now that when my plants die, it won't be from overwatering.

DIEFFENBACHIA
Arum or Calla Family
(Dieffenbachia)

The dieffenbachia is one of the most popular of indoor plants. It comes in many varieties, a favorite being *Dieffenbachia picta,* which has light green leaves with darker ribs and borders. *D. amoena* is a very large plant that can grow to over six feet tall with enormous leaves.

My beautiful dieffenbachia happens to be sitting right next to my ill-fated dracaena—the one used by the kitten as a climbing post. Having shredded most of the bottom leaves from the dracaena, Solomon decided that he was going on to better things.

He attacked the dieffenbachia, and he must have bitten into its stem, because the next thing I saw was a frantic kitten running around rubbing his nose on the carpet and pushing at it with his paws. Since then he has learned to stay away from the dieffenbachia. It's not by chance that its nickname is "dumb cane," because its bitter juice can bring on a partial paralysis of the tongue.

A dieffenbachia is a good plant to practice all your propagation tricks on. It has the unfortunate habit of losing all its bottom leaves (even without their being pulled off by a four-footed creature).

Tip cutting

When your plant is young and has a soft stem, you can cut off the topknot of leaves with four inches of stem and root it in water. Stand the stem in a small bottle of water in bright light. In a few weeks roots will form, and you can pot the cutting in soil.

Crock a three-inch pot and fill it with potting soil. Make a hole in the center of the potting soil for the cutting. Insert the cutting and gently press the soil around the edge of the pot, taking care not to injure the roots.

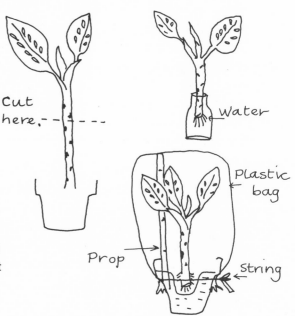

46

To prevent shock, your plant should be watered with a vitamin B₁ solution. You can also put the plant into a plastic-bag greenhouse for a few days until the danger of wilting has passed. Don't forget to harden it up before taking it out of the greenhouse.

Air layering

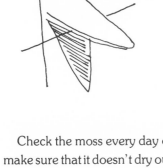

Cut held open with toothpick

Older dieffenbachias develop thick woody stems, and these have to be air layered.

Make a cut three-quarters of the way through the stem at an angle of 45 degrees, just above the place where you want the new roots to form. Insert a toothpick into the cut to prevent it from healing itself shut. Take a handful of sphagnum moss which has been soaked in water and wrung out, and wrap it around the stem. Now cover the moss with a sheet of plastic wrap and tie it at top and bottom with Twist-ems. It should be tight enough to prevent the moss from slipping down the stem.

Check the moss every day or so to make sure that it doesn't dry out. If it's dry, add water with a household meat baster by untying the top Twist-em and dripping the water on the moss. Roots will appear through the moss, and the stem should be cut just below the roots. Discard the plastic wrap, and plant the whole root ball in a pot of soil.

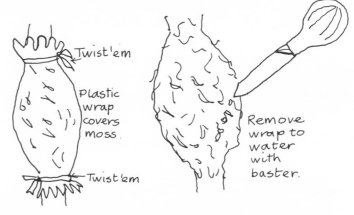

Twist'em

Plastic wrap covers moss.

Twist'em

Remove wrap to water with baster.

Stem cutting

You will be left with a long, scarred stem which can be cut into three-inch pieces. Dust their cut ends with fungicide.

Fill a shallow pot half-full of prepared vermiculite. Lay the pieces of stem half-buried in a horizontal position. Cover the pot with plastic wrap tied under the lip of the pot with string.

It is necessary to have bottom heat when making stem cuttings, so set the pot on the yogurt maker. Eventually a shoot will appear from one of the "eyes" on the stem. When it is an inch tall, take it off the yogurt maker and harden it up. Plant each section of stem in a separate pot.

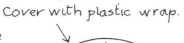

Cover with plastic wrap.

Soil level

string

YOGURT

DONATIONS AND GIFTS:
CHRYSANTHEMUMS AND AZALEAS

Chrysanthemums and azaleas are often given as gifts. Both have a short but memorable blooming period, then look as if they are about to die, so you throw them out. If you have the right conditions, you can hang on to them and they will bloom again. You can also take cuttings from them to make new plants.

CHRYSANTHEMUM   Composite Family
(Chrysanthemum morifolium or C. hortorum)

Once the flowers have died, cut the plant down to a couple of inches. The condition you will have to provide is somewhere colder than the house but not colder than 45 degrees. Put your plant in this unheated area, where it can still get light, and water it very sparingly—a scant cup a week.

As soon as the warm spring weather arrives, your plant will start producing vigorous growth. Take tip cuttings that have at least three nodes. They will root easily in water. When rooted, plant them in soil, taking the precautions mentioned on page 7, which are providing a greenhouse and watering with a vitamin B_1 solution.

The mother plant can be taken back into the house and given good light and regular feedings. Pot her up in a larger pot at the first sign of being pot-bound. (See page 109.)

You must prune the cuttings ruthlessly, pinching them back whenever they start growing too tall, in order to produce a bushy plant.

Winter

Spring

AZALEA   (Azalea)   Heath Family

Azalea plants will flower longer indoors if you keep them in a cool room. When the flowers have died, pick them off and take tip cuttings from the soft wood stems (those that are flexible and green). Soak some sphagnum moss in water, wring it out and wrap each stem in a nest, as you do in air layering. Cover it with plastic wrap and tie the top and bottom with Twist-ems. Make sure that the moss does not dry out. Put the stems and root balls into a plastic-bag greenhouse for six to eight weeks. When they have rooted, harden them up before planting each stem and root ball in potting soil.

Azaleas need to be kept cool during the summer, so a shady porch would do fine. They must be kept cool (50 degrees) in the autumn; and, if brought indoors in December, they will think it is spring and form flowers. They should be fed well at this time and kept moist. They also appreciate being misted during their flowering period.

Put it into a plastic bag for six to eight weeks.

DONKEY'S TAIL *(Sedum morganianum)* Stonecrop Family

Donkey's tail is one of 300 varieties of sedum. (Other members of the Crassula branch of the stonecrop family are echeveria and kalanchoe, both very popular plants.) Donkey's tail looks at its best when hanging up so that the "tails" can droop over the sides of the pot. It is a very fragile plant, though, and each stem is made up of hundreds of fleshy "knobs" that break off at the slightest touch.

Tip cuttings

All that you need to propagate this plant is to have one generous or two myopic friends. First, steal ten pieces. Each piece should be about six inches in length. Make a one-inch stem by removing one inch of fleshy knobs above the place where you broke it off.

Crock a very shallow hanging pot and fill it with a mixture of three-quarters sand and one-quarter potting soil. You are creating a fast-draining soil, as sedums do not like to have wet feet.

Carefully push the stems, spaced evenly, into the soil. Water well to settle the soil. Hang your plant in a window where it will receive bright light.

As your plant grows, it will fill out at the soil level and over a period of years will become a lovely full plant. But do not expect anything to happen fast as this is a very slow grower.

It is now three years since I did my first thieving, and the pot is looking so full that I suppose it's about time I shared some of my bounty with my friends.

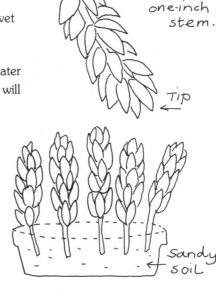

Break off knobs to make a one-inch stem.

Tip

sandy soil

49

DRACAENA   *(Dracaena)*   Lily Family

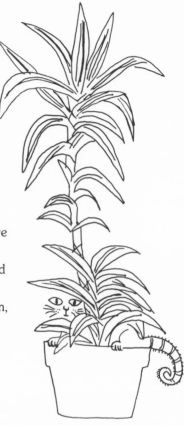

Dracaenas are very popular plants and with excellent reason, as they can be grown indoors very successfully and are capable of growing very tall.

I have, living in my dracaena, a breed of pest not usually mentioned in plant books. It has a pink nose and four paws and was abandoned in the street. I found him living under the cars when he was three months old—so can you blame me? His name is Solomon Eagle.

The first week he lived in the dracaena, hidden by its protective leaves, and I would see that naughty little face peering out at me from behind the leaves. The second week he realized that he could climb up the stems, and from then on it was good-bye dracaena. I decided that as I didn't really want a palm tree in my living room, I would have to air-layer it.

Toothpick holds cut open.

Twist 'em →

← Plastic wrap

water

New roots appear through moss.

Sever stem below roots.

Air layering

Make a cut three-quarters of the way through the stem at an angle of 45 degrees, just above where you want the new roots to form. Insert a toothpick into the cut to prevent it from sealing itself shut. Take a handful of sphagnum moss that has been soaked in water and wrung out, and wrap it around the cut stem. Now cover the moss with plastic wrap and tie it at the top and bottom with Twist-ems, tightly enough to prevent the moss from slipping down the stem.

Check the moss frequently to make sure that it doesn't dry and add water by dripping it from a household meat baster onto the moss. When roots appear through the moss, cut the stem just below the roots. Remove the plastic wrap, then plant the whole root ball in a pot of soil.

Tip cutting

If your dracaena is only a small one and not large enough to air layer, you can cut off its topknot and make a tip cutting. With a sharp knife, cut off the topknot of leaves with four inches of stem. Stand the stem in a small bottle of water in bright light. In a few weeks roots will be well enough formed to pot in potting soil.

Crock a small pot and fill it with potting soil. Make a hole in the center of the soil and gently insert your rooted cutting into the hole, pressing the soil carefully around the roots. Water with a vitamin B₁ solution to help prevent shock.

Don't throw away your old plants after decapitating them because sometimes new shoots form just below the stub and in time these become a new plant. If, on the other hand, you have air layered your old dracaena, you will be left with about a yard of bare stem, which adds nothing to its beauty.

Roots form easily in water.

Put a jam jar over the new plant to prevent wilting.

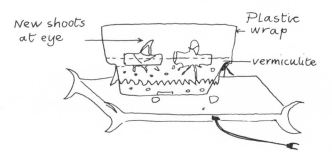

New shoots at eye

Plastic wrap

vermiculite

Stem cutting

Cut the stem into three- or four-inch pieces and dust their cut ends with fungicide.

New plant

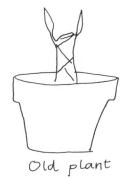

Old plant

Fill a shallow pot half-full of prepared vermiculite. Place the pieces of stem in a horizontal position, half-buried in the vermiculite. Cover the pot with plastic wrap tied under the lip with string.

You need bottom heat when trying to induce an old stem to put out new shoots, so set the pot on the yogurt maker. Eventually a shoot will appear from one of the "eyes." When it is an inch tall, take it off the yogurt maker and harden it up. Each piece of stem can be planted in its own pot.

ECHEVERIA   *(Echeveria)*   Stonecrop Family

Echeverias come from the Crassula branch of the Stonecrop Family, other cousins being sedums and kalanchoes. They have thick fleshy leaves and pretty flowers that grow in clusters. Two popular varieties are *Echeveria elegans,* which has a silver-gray rosette of leaves with pink or orange flowers, and *E. pulvinata,* which has fat scarlet-edged leaves and red flowers. They are strong plants and are easy to propagate, either from offsets or single leaves. The following story will give you some idea as to how hardy they are.

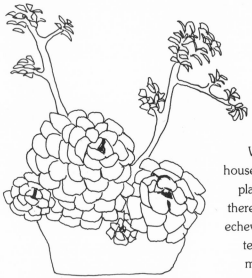

Echeveria elegans

I have an Irish friend called Connell, and when she first moved out to California, she was overwhelmed at the marvelous plants growing in her garden. Echeverias are quite rare in the United Kingdom, but are very common in California, as most of them come from Mexico.

When she and her husband had to move to another house, she packed two seed boxes full of echeverias and planted them in her new garden. Since the first move, there have been two more, and each time she dug up the echeverias and took them with her. Last time there were ten seed boxes rather than two. The echeverias have multiplied happily and now, in their final home, they grow everywhere—in the garden, in the house, hanging from the beams.

As you can see, these plants are very unneurotic and propagate themselves easily at any opportunity. So if you simply have to move house, just pack them up and take them along with the rest of your belongings.

Echeverias put out offsets at the base of the mother plant. These can be pulled off gently and repotted in a mixture of three-quarters horticultural sand and one-quarter potting soil. *E. pulv-oliver,* which forms rosettes at the end of thick stems, can be cut off with two inches of stem and rooted in the same sandy soil. Echeverias appreciate your best window and need to be kept fairly dry when mature.

E. pulv-oliver

Offsets can be pulled off.

52

FIDDLE-LEAF FIG *(Ficus lyrata or F. pandurata)* Fig Family

I was driving along the road the other day and out of the corner of my eye I saw this enormous fiddle-leaf fig towering over its neighbors. I had to laugh because this is one of those trees that you buy as a charming young plant, and it grows and grows until in most cases you are either forced to give it to a friend with a high ceiling or plant it in the garden and pray that it will survive the winter.

It is related to the rubber plant and receives its name from its violin-shaped leaves. As with other rubber plants, fiddle-leaf figs are inclined to grow very tall, often on a single stem; if you are lucky, however, your plant may branch by putting out side shoots. These shoots can be cut off close to the stem and will root in water. It is always well to remember that plants root twice as fast when in bright light.

Air Layer here.

Air layering

If, however, your tree is reaching the ceiling, you will probably be better off air layering it two or three feet from the top. This amputation may, in turn, force side shoots to appear lower down on the mother plant, which will give it a better appearance.

Toothpick

You will have to strip away one or two leaves from the stem in order to give yourself the three or four inches of space you need to air layer your plant.

Plastic wrap

Roots appear through moss.

Make a cut three-quarters of the way through the stem at an angle of 45 degrees. Insert a toothpick into the cut to prevent it from sealing itself shut. Wrap the cut in a handful of sphagnum moss which was soaked in water and then wrung out. Wrap this, in turn, in plastic and tie it at the top and bottom with Twist-ems; make sure it is tight enough to prevent the moss from slipping down the stem. The roots will appear through the moss. When they are one inch long, cut the stem just below the roots. Discard the plastic wrap and plant the whole root ball in a pot of soil.

While the roots are forming, check the moss regularly to see that it hasn't dried out. To add more water, use a kitchen meat baster, dripping the water onto the moss.

If you have a large fig plant, make sure that its pot is big enough for it. If roots appear above the surface, this indicates that your plant needs more space. A root-bound fig makes watering difficult, as this is a plant that loses its bottom leaves for exactly the opposite reason that other plants lose theirs—*because it is not getting enough water.* Ice cubes will take care of this problem because their slow rate of melting allows full absorption by the roots. However, it would be better to transfer your plant to a larger pot (unless you have an automatic ice-maker).

Water→

Untie plastic wrap and top twist 'em.

Tip cutting

You may find that your plant's stem is not thick enough to air layer, having the thin green stem common to young plants rather than the thick woody stem of an older plant. If this is the case, you can cut it off as a tip cutting and root it in water. Cut the stem with at least three nodes, place it upright in water, and be sure that the water covers a node, as that is where new roots will form.

However, remember that a water-rooted plant presents a problem when it is transferred to soil because it has to acclimatize itself to the new growing medium. A way to avoid this is by using a "two-stage" pot.

Peat pot filled with vermiculite is inserted into center of bulb pot.

"Two-stage" pot

Fill a small peat pot with prepared vermiculite and insert it into the center of a bulb pot filled with potting soil. The tip cutting goes into the peat pot.

As long as you keep the vermiculite damp, roots will form and travel through the peat pot into the potting soil. The action of the water will cause the peat pot to break down after a while and act as a fertilizer for the potting soil.

Although the two-stage pot is more normally used when rooting fragile-stemmed plants that break when being transplanted, it can actually be used for any cutting that forms roots in vermiculite.

When you are next given a fiddle-leaf fig, be prepared for a fast grower. Until someone hybridizes a miniature fig, you are going to have to cut it back regularly.

FITTONIA   *(Fittonia verschaffeltii)*   Acanthus Family

Fittonia is a most beautiful little plant that is often used in terrariums, as it loves humidity. *Fittonia verschaffeltii* is the most commonly found species, and *F. verschaffeltii argyroneura* (meaning white-veined) is the most popular variety.

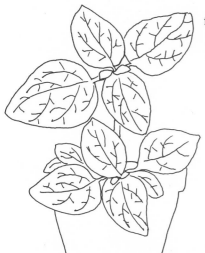

People often ask me how plants get their botanical names. The fittonia was named after Elizabeth and Sarah Fitton, two Victorian ladies who wrote *Conversations on Botany* in mid–nineteenth-century England.

It is a great honor to have a plant named after you, so one must appreciate the work of these two ladies at a time when it was not popular for women to be professional at anything besides being wives.

This little plant benefits from being pinched back frequently, because it is inclined to grow leggy. It requires humidity to flourish, so cuttings grow very happily in water.

Tip cuttings

Break off tip cuttings with at least two pairs of leaves. Stand the stems in a small bottle of water—small aspirin bottles are perfect—and roots will form very rapidly.

When potting a water-rooted cutting, take the necessary precautions against wilting.

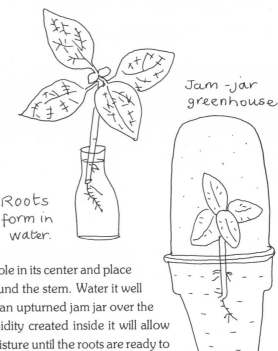

Jam-jar greenhouse

Roots form in water.

Crock a small pot and fill it with soil. Make a hole in its center and place the rooted cutting in it. Press the soil gently around the stem. Water it well with a vitamin B_1 solution and immediately put an upturned jam jar over the pot. This provides a greenhouse, and the humidity created inside it will allow the leaves to breathe in some of the required moisture until the roots are ready to take over. Don't forget to harden up your plant slowly.

FLAME VIOLET   *(Episcia)*   Gesneriad Family

Flame violet, a prettily leaved plant related to the African violet and gloxinia, is best as a hanging plant. Its runners trail below the pot and, if left uncut, grow into beautiful masses of leaves. Its Greek name, *episkia,* meaning "shady," refers to its light preference.

It is an ideal plant for growing indoors. However, a shady garden is not the same as a dark house, so your plant will do best on a bright windowsill where it does not receive direct sunlight.

I tend to think of this plant as being "disposable" because once it has passed its prime, it serves as a mother plant for tip cuttings. Then when it gets too old and ungainly, I get rid of it and concentrate my attention on the children.

The most popular species is *Episcia cupreata,* which comes in many beautiful varieties: *E. lilacina* 'Cuprea' with bronze leaves and lavender flowers; *E. punctata* with green leaves and purple flowers; and *E. cupreata* 'Acajou' with variegated leaves and an orange flower.

The *Episcia cupreata* is easy to propagate because it throws out runners. You can either pin them down in a small pot next to the mother plant or cut them off and root them in water. When the roots are one to two inches long, pot them in soil.

You can also take tip cuttings any time the plant needs to be pinched back. These will form roots in water, and four or five cuttings potted together will give you a full plant.

Episcia cupreata 'Acajou'

Runner, pinned down in small pot

This plant's growing cycle includes a dormant period. When your plant appears to be dying, remove it from its bright window, cut off any old leggy stems and withered flowers, and withhold water gradually until you are giving it a scant cupful a week. After two months new shoots will appear, and this is your signal that its dormant period is over and it is ready to face the world. Put it back onto the windowsill and water regularly.

As a relative of the African violet, episcia has definite likes and dislikes. It likes a moist soil and it dislikes a dry atmosphere, so be sure to water and mist it regularly. However, thank heavens it is not nearly so persnickety as the African violet and therefore much easier to please.

56

FLAMINGO FLOWER   Arum or Calla Family
(Anthurium)

This is a member of one of the largest families of house-plants, and you will immediately recognize this plant's flowers even if you have seen them used only in dried flower arrangements. The bright red spathe-type flowers are quite spectacular and look as if they have been varnished. It is hard to believe that they grow this way.

Because their natural habitat is the tropical forest, a window that does not receive direct sunshine suits them very well. They should be constantly misted and watered.

The flamingo flower is botanically known as *Anthurium andreanum.* It is rather confusing as a cousin, *A. scherzerianum,* is also called flamingo flower, depending upon which reference book you use. However, both are grown for their superb flowers, and two others, *A. crystallinum* and *A. veitchii,* are grown for their beautiful leaves.

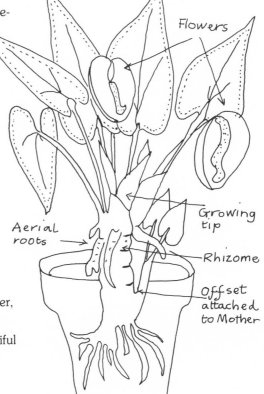

Flowers

Aerial roots

Growing tip

Rhizome

Offset attached to Mother

Jam-jar greenhouse

Tilt

Pebble

A. andreanum grows from a central upright rhizome which puts out aerial roots that hang down. The best way to propagate this plant is to remove suckers that form at the soil level. Gently knock the plant out of its pot and separate the sucker from the mother plant. You will find that they share the same roots, so you will have to cut it away from its mother. Crock a small pot of potting soil and plant your sucker. Cover it with a jam jar for a few days until the danger of wilting is over. Water with a vitamin B_1 solution.

Harden up your small plant by tipping the jam jar little by little until the air inside the jar is at the same temperature and humidity levels as that outside.

FUCHSIA *(Fuchsia)* Evening-Primrose Family

The fuchsia is named after the great German botanist Leonhard Fuchs, who, in 1542, produced one of the most beautiful books ever printed; *De Historia Stirpium,* consisting of over 500 full-page woodcuts of plants. He is certainly well remembered through the plant that bears his name.

There is an infinity of fuchsias now available—single flowers, doubles, white, pink, red, a mixture of all three; some with ruffles like a ballerina's tutu; those that climb up and, particularly for us, those that hang down, which make perfect plants for hanging in a bright, sunny window.

Fuchsias are very easy to propagate; in fact, in my grandparents' time people used to throw away the mother plant and just keep the cuttings. However, you needn't be quite so drastic as long as you remember that fuchsias must be cut back severely at the end of their blooming season, or they will grow very leggy.

Although some fuchsias never seem to know when the blooming season is over, going on and on producing beautiful flowers, generally they stop blooming by winter—unless you have them growing under a plant lamp, in which case they go on forever, in eternal summer.

Fuchsia 'Whitemost'

To cut back your fuchsia, you must prune each stem right back to the woody main stem. This often means that your plant will be denuded of leaves, but don't worry as the new growth will start up again after one to two months of rest. Take your bare plant away from its bright perch and put it into a shady spot. Gradually cut down on the watering so that you end up giving it a scant cupful a week. This change of atmosphere allows your plant to become dormant.

A good cutting

Tip cuttings

You are left with an armful of cuttings, and it takes a very cold heart not to be dismayed at throwing most of them out. But unless you want to start a nursery, ten cuttings is all you really need because each cutting will become a new plant.

Take your tip cuttings with at least three pairs of leaves. Try to find stems that are firm enough to stand upright without a prop. Five cuttings can be rooted together in one six-inch pot. Crock your pot and fill it with prepared vermiculite. Make a hole for each cutting with a thin stick and insert the stems. Water with a vitamin B_1 solution for the first week.

Prop for plastic bag

Fuchsias need humidity in order to root, so make a greenhouse with a plastic bag. If you have only one or two cuttings, each can go into a separate small pot covered with a jam jar.

Fuchsias take quite a long time to form good strong roots, so be prepared to leave them rooting for two months. Don't forget to harden them up before taking them out of the greenhouse. You can plant each cutting in its own four-inch pot or, if you prefer, you can plant a few of them together in a basket. (For instructions on how to make up a basket, see page 114.) The advantage of planting young cuttings together in a basket is that you appear to have a full and bushy plant instead of a young thin one.

Jam jar over single cutting

Meanwhile, the mother plant has been sitting quietly by herself working up energy for the coming season. As soon as you notice new leaves appearing, put her back into the sunny window and commence watering and fertilizing regularly. When fuchsias are in bloom, they have to be fertilized twice a month; at other times, except during dormancy, once a month is adequate. Watch your plant for signs of wilting and make up your own watering schedule, as every plant has special needs. Don't forget to remove dead heads during the blooming season, or your plant will use up all her energy producing seeds.

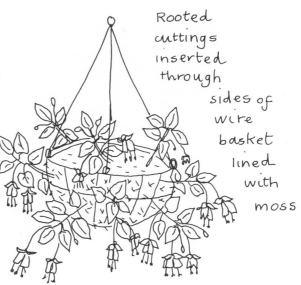

Rooted cuttings inserted through sides of wire basket lined with moss

GERANIUMS *(Pelargonium hortorum)* Geranium Family

There are over 8,000 varieties of geraniums, which can be broken down roughly into the following categories:

Regals

These fancy-leaf pelargoniums include the Martha Washington varieties, plants with heart-shaped crinkly leaves and large, beautiful, showy multi-colored flowers.

Zonals

These comprise the common garden geraniums; they have round leaves and flowers with single, semidouble or double petals.

Ivy Leaf

These geraniums are most often used in window boxes or baskets, as they trail so spectacularly. Their leaves are ivy-shaped. Their flowers are singles or doubles.

Scented Leaf

There are over 200 varieties, the most popular being lemon-scented or rose-scented. I have an unusual apricot-scented geranium with a lovely rose-colored flower.

Single

Semi-double

Double

We all know that geraniums do marvelously outdoors, where they receive sunshine during the day and cool temperatures at night. But bring them indoors and you're heading for trouble unless you learn how to compensate.

Light is a problem because geraniums need at least a couple of hours of sun, and more if possible. This is almost impossible to achieve indoors unless you have large bay windows or skylights. If you don't you will have to use a plant light. A plant day of sixteen hours (8 A.M. to midnight) is the equivalent to light from a sunny garden. So when you get up in the morning, turn on the light and leave it on until you go to bed.

The second problem with indoor geranium growing is that most houses are far too warm for them at night. Outdoors, the temperature drops immediately when the sun sets, so you have to try to create a similar condition inside. A good method is to put them under plant lights during the day, but move them onto a windowsill with the window open at night. They shouldn't get cooler than 60 degrees; in the winter, just turning off the heat might be enough. This is going to wreak havoc with your thermostat; but if you want indoor geraniums, you'll just have to make some sacrifices!

One-year-old geranium cuttings are fine for the house, but because they have a way of getting very big very quickly, I have taken to growing dwarf geraniums indoors. These are charming little plants that rarely grow more than twelve inches tall and bear beautiful large flowers. I am always surprised at the size of their blooms.

I have a 'Mrs. Doyden' dwarf geranium in a three-inch pot. It is only three inches tall, but its flower is four inches in diameter on an eight-inch stem!

There are many popular dwarf geraniums, with charming names—a whole Snow White and dwarf series; a planetary series including 'Saturn' and 'Jupiter'; and others such as 'Redondo,' 'Rusty' and 'Lady Plymouth.' Another beautiful dwarf geranium species is *Geranium erodium*, a tiny little plant whose lavender flowers look like purple buttercups and bloom for only one day.

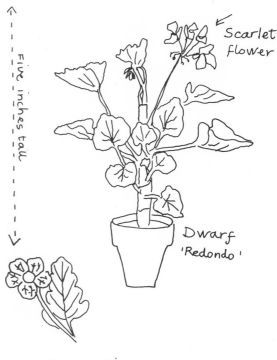

Five inches tall

Scarlet flower

Dwarf 'Redondo'

Geranium erodium

Tip cuttings

Tip cuttings are taken for all forms of geraniums. I make my cuttings in the autumn when my plants have stopped flowering and are beginning to look "leggy." I cut back their stems severely to give them a more compact look, and this leaves me with a lot of tip cuttings.

When I have plenty of clay pots, I use prepared vermiculite as a rooting medium. But if I have only plastic pots, I use a different rooting medium, one made up of three-quarters sand and one-quarter potting soil. The reason that I don't use vermiculite in plastic pots is that they are not porous and cannot "breathe", and the vermiculite stays so wet that algae often form on its surface. This deprives the cutting of oxygen, and it rots and dies. So remember, if you have run out of clay pots, it's safer to use a mixture of sand and soil.

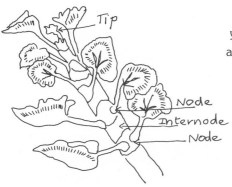

Tip

Node

Internode

Node

Snap off the long stems from the mother plant. Now take your sharp knife and wipe it with a cotton swab dipped in alcohol to prevent any disease from being transmitted from plant to plant.

Crock and fill your pots. A three-inch pot is a very good size for a young cutting. Look at the stem and you will see that it consists of sections called nodes. The area between the nodes is called the "internode."

Count down three nodes from the tip of the leaves. Make your cut one-eighth of an inch below the third node. Roll the stem around as you make the cut to prevent it from being squashed. Remove any leaves from the second and third nodes. Dip the cut end in a hormone-rooting powder.

Take a pencil and make a hole in your rooting medium. Put your cutting into the hole deep enough to cover the third node. Press the rooting medium gently around the stem to hold it upright. Water it now and for the first week with a vitamin B_1 solution as an antishock treatment.

If you are out of small pots, you can root three or four cuttings together in a larger pot. Just make sure that their leaves don't touch. And if you have a lot of cuttings, root them in a seed box at two-inch intervals.

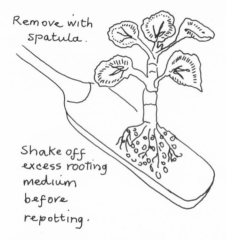

Your cuttings will root in about six weeks. A slight resistance to a gentle tug will tell you that roots have formed. Take a spatula and lift each cutting carefully out of the rooting mix, trying to avoid breaking off any roots. Make up a soil mix consisting of three-quarters soil and one-quarter sand.

Crock a three-inch pot and put one inch of the soil mix into the bottom. Hold the cutting in the pot with one hand and, with the other, add more soil until the pot is filled. Press the soil around the edges of the pot, but not directly on the roots or you might break them. Bang the pot gently a couple of times to settle the soil, then water it with a vitamin B_1 solution as an antishock treatment.

This small pot will be your cutting's home for its first year. Geraniums like to be pot-bound and flower more profusely when their roots are squashed in a small area. Fertilize your young plant with a solution of regular fertilizer that is one-quarter to one-eighth as strong as usual.

Geraniums need to be pinched back (page 10) to encourage the lower leaves to branch out and become bushy. Pinch off the new growth with your finger and thumb. Geraniums should be kept on the dry side—this is why sand is added to their growing medium. During the blooming period they benefit from monthly fertilization, but during the winter, when they are semidormant, omit it. Start it up again when you see the spring growth appearing.

62

GLOXINIA *(Sinningia speciosa)* Gesneriad Family

The gloxinia is a wonderfully showy plant that someone is sure to give you as a gift. It is immediately recognizable by its trumpet-shaped flowers of many sizes and colors: single trumpets; "slipper-flowered" blooms of white, yellow or lavender; and double trumpets, frilly or ruffled, in red, white, blue and speckled.

Gloxinia 'Mont Blanc'

The gloxinia grows from a tuber and has a dormant period after blooming. If you aren't aware of this, you may think that you've done it again—murdered your poor plant, in spite of the care and attention you were giving it. Don't worry. A gloxinia puts on a fantastic flower show and then needs time to recover.

The first indication that dormancy is approaching is that your plant stops putting out buds or new leaves. At this stage, slowly cut back on watering. When the leaves begin to wither, remove the plant from its bright perch and cut off all the old leaves and withered flowers. A tuber in its dormancy likes to be where it is cool, so if you have an unheated porch where the temperature is about 45 degrees, put it there. A tuber, like a potato, carries its food supply around with it, so you have to give it only enough water to prevent it from shriveling up—a scant cupful every two weeks. Pour the water around the sides of the pot, not directly on the tuber, as you don't want it to rot.

After a rest of one to two months, new shoots will appear on the tuber. At this sign, take your plant from its resting place and repot it in fresh soil. Once new growth appears, you can resume watering your plant—it likes to be kept fairly moist. It does not require direct sunshine but does best in bright light—and stupendously under a plant light.

New growth appears from eyes in spring.

63

Leaf cuttings

Like its cousin the African violet, the easiest
way to propagate your gloxinia is by leaf cuttings.

Take a firm young leaf, lay it on its face, and make a series of
cuts through its main veins. Crock a shallow pot and half fill it
with prepared vermiculite, leaving a gap of two inches between
the vermiculite and the top of the pot. Place the leaf with its
underside down on top of the vermiculite. If the leaf pops up,
weight it down with some marbles or pebbles. It can be further
secured by inserting hairpins into the cuts.

Ye olde ● yogurt maker

Cover the pot with plastic wrap tied
under the lip of the pot with string. There
should be enough room for the young
shoots to form under the plastic wrap
without touching their heads, so half fill
the pot with vermiculite.

Set the pot on the yogurt maker, as it is essential to have bottom heat when rooting leaf
cuttings. If you do not have a yogurt maker, any source of constant mild heat will
substitute—in a pinch, even the pilot light of your gas stove will do, though it might present
problems whenever you need to cook dinner!

Small plantlets will slowly form at the cuts; when
they have at least two pairs of leaves, they can be
gently picked up from the vermiculite and potted in
small pots of their own

When a lot of plants are in a greenhouse and
only one of them is ready to leave it, you can't
harden it up in the usual manner. In this case, get
your small pot ready for the cutting, whiz it out of
the greenhouse into its own pot, and plonk a jam jar
down over its head—all within the space of thirty
seconds! Set the little pot back on the yogurt maker
for a day or two, until you see that your plantlet is
not wilting. Harden it up slowly by tilting the jar
more and more each day.

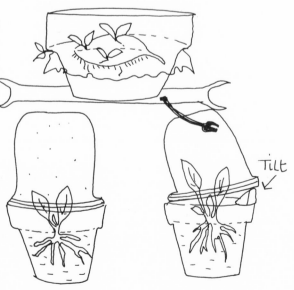

Tilt

64

GRAPE IVY   *(Cissus rhombifolia)*   Grape Family

This is one of those marvelous plants that is like a favorite spinster aunt: always there when needed and totally undemanding. Grape ivy adds color and shine to any corner. Its dark green leaves are an indication that it will accept whatever light you have available, and it does not *demand* to be in the limelight.

I am also fond of grape ivy because it needs regular pinching back. And each piece that has been pinched can be rooted in water to make another plant.

If you put two or three cuttings together in a glass on a windowsill, they will root together. You can pot them together to give you a fuller plant.

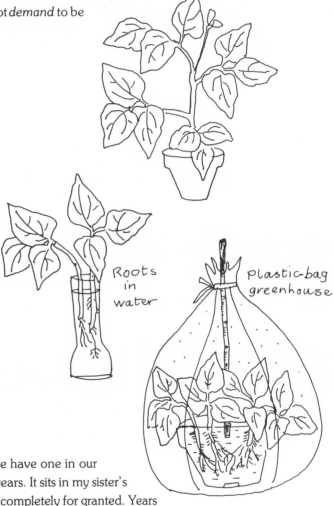

Roots in water

plastic-bag greenhouse

When the roots are one inch long, crock a four-inch pot and fill it with potting soil. Make a hole in the center of the soil for the roots. Put in your cuttings and press the soil carefully around the stems. The roots will sort themselves out under the surface.

Put the pot into a plastic-bag greenhouse for a few days as a precaution against wilting and water it with a solution of vitamin B_1 as an antishock treatment.

Grape ivy can grow to an enormous size. We have one in our family that has been around for at least fifteen years. It sits in my sister's living room in a pewter coal scuttle and is taken completely for granted. Years ago it was trained to grow on a trellis, and it is now over seven feet tall. I once asked my sister what on earth she did to keep it so healthy and glossy. She looked rather surprised and said, "Absolutely nothing."

That is why I love this plant. While I am fussing around with the African violets and begonias, measuring fertilizer and making sure I haven't splashed water on their wretched leaves, my grape ivy doesn't hold it against me if I forget to water it. If not today, then tomorrow—it can wait.

IMPATIENS

(Impatiens holstii)   Balsam Family

In America impatiens is known as "patient Lucy," while in Europe the name is "busy Lizzie." Whatever its name, this is a marvelous plant to propagate. In general, there seem to be two varieties: those that grow up with thick sturdy stems, and those that spread with thin spindly stems. You must be very fussy about those first cuttings, so it's worth looking around to find a really strong mother plant. These are usually found growing outside, where they learn to be hardier. Look for a thick fleshy stem and dark green leaves as signs of strength.

My first cuttings came from a friend who got hers from Catalina Island off the California mainland, where the plant had learned to brave the hot sun and sea breezes. Now, two years later, it has completely taken over the garden, has filled countless numbers of hanging pots and has provided all my friends with their cuttings.

stem will also grow roots.

Break off six inches of tip.

There are two ways to propagate this plant, both equally successful.

Tip cuttings in water

Break off the tip with about six inches of stem. If your plants have grown very tall, you can break the stems into sections and these will root also. Put the cuttings into a bottle of water in bright light. Sometimes the cuttings get slimy and you have to throw them out, but generally, if you have a good, lusty mother plant, you will have happy, cheerful children with thick stems that will root in approximately two weeks.

66

Wait until the roots are at least one inch long before potting them in soil. Two or three stems together in a six-inch pot will provide you with a marvelous plant. Pinch them back constantly during their early stages of growth, as this forces them to branch out lower down on the stem and to form new stems at soil level. Water-rooted cuttings always wilt when being transferred to soil, so water your plant with a vitamin B₁ solution as an antishock treatment and put it into a plastic-bag greenhouse immediately. It will revive in a few days. Harden up the plant slowly.

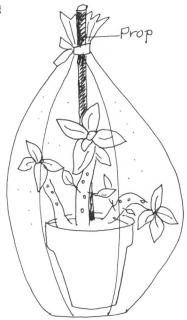

Prop

Tip cuttings in the "two-stage" pot

Fill a small peat pot with prepared vermiculite and insert it into a wide bulb pot filled with potting soil. The tip cuttings go into the vermiculite, which must be kept constantly moist. Put the double pot into a plastic-bag greenhouse. The stems will wilt for the first few days, but they will adjust to their new home and slowly pull themselves up. As soon as their stems are rigid again, they can be hardened up. The cuttings will form roots in the vermiculite and gradually grow through the peat pot into the potting soil. The peat pot will slowly break down and add nourishment to the potting soil.

The advantage to using this pot is that you don't have to repot the cuttings. The two-stage pot is their permanent home. They should also be pinched back regularly to make them thick. They will do much better if they can get some sunshine because the number of flowers they bear is in direct proportion to the amount of sunshine they get. If they show no signs of flowering, put them under a plant light and see the difference.

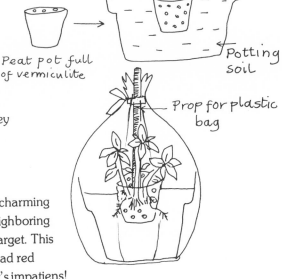

Peat pot is inserted into bulb pot.

Peat pot full of vermiculite

Potting soil

Prop for plastic bag

Their botanical name *Impatiens* alludes to their charming habit of *impatiently* seeding themselves in their neighboring pots. Any plant within their proximity becomes a target. This year, a surprised Creeping Charlie found that he had red flowers owing to his close relationship with last year's impatiens!

They are very much beloved by snails because of their fleshy succulent stems—so if you ever put them outside, watch out!

67

IVY   *(Hedera helix)*   Ginseng Family

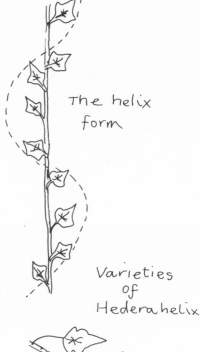

The helix form

Varieties of Hedera helix

The ivy that is most commonly grown indoors is called English ivy, and it comes in many varieties and colors. Ivy grows in a geometrical form known as a helix (from the Greek word meaning spiral), and this term is included in its botanical name, *Hedera helix,* written as *H. h.* The helix occurs throughout nature—even in the genetic code of human beings, where it takes the form of a double helix.

I am sure that I am not alone in having bought a beautiful pot of miniature ivy, glossy and green and hanging down over its pot in a most decorative way, only to see it start losing its leaves a month later. When I first saw its leaf edges crinkling up from what I presumed was a lack of water, I ended up drowning it. I comforted myself by saying that ivy was an outdoor plant anyway, so imagining that it would do well indoors was a conspiracy devised by plant shops. Then I went into someone else's house and found that it was doing beautifully there. It's so easy to get an inferiority complex when you are growing plants!

It's the warmth of our houses that does our ivy in. Those telltale brown tips to the leaves are a sign that it is not getting enough humidity. Spray it with water every day. Light is another problem because it needs excellent light. Use a plant lamp if you are not sure about your home's light.

H.h. 'Pittsburgh'

H.h. cordata

H.h. 'Weber's California'

H. h. baltica

There are over seventy varieties of ivy to choose from. The most popular is Hahn's miniature branching ivy, with pretty, tiny leaves which are dark green. The granddaddy of all miniature ivies is *H. h. hibernica* from Ireland. *H. h.* 'Pittsburgh' is the son of Irish ivy and the father of almost all other miniature ivies. *H. h. cordata* has heart-shaped leaves growing closely together. *H. h.* 'Weber's California' is a miniature ivy used in terrariums. *H. h. baltica* has small five-lobed leaves.

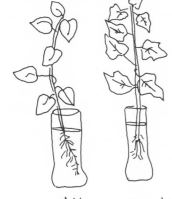

Cuttings root in water.

Rooting in water

If you have a bright windowsill, your cuttings will root in a week or two. Under a plant light, they will root even faster.

Take cuttings with at least three or four leaves and stand them in small bottles of water. In a couple of weeks you can pot them.

Crock a four-inch pot and fill it with potting soil. Make holes with a stick and insert three or four rooted cuttings into the same pot. This gives a fuller-looking plant. Press the soil carefully around the stems.

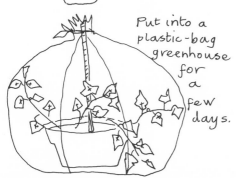

Put into a plastic-bag greenhouse for a few days.

As with all water-rooted cuttings, you must be very careful to prevent wilting when transferring them from water to their new environment. At this stage use a vitamin B_1 solution as an antishock treatment when you water your plant and cover the pot with a plastic-bag greenhouse. After a few days, if the leaves show no sign of wilting harden up your plant by slowly tearing holes in the plastic bag.

Rooting in sand

Fill a shallow container with sand and lay your ivy cuttings horizontally across it. Pin them down with hairpins. Keep the sand damp. New branches will form from each leaf, and this is a good way to cover a large area quickly.

After a few weeks, give the cuttings a gentle tug; if you feel a resistance, this means that roots have formed. Transfer your cuttings to potting soil. Three or four cuttings in a wide, shallow pot will give you a very full plant in quite a short time.

Pinned to the sand

Roots form at contact.

69

JADE PLANT *(Crassula argentea)* Stonecrop Family

The jade plant, known as the Japanese rubber plant, grows like a sturdy little tree and has a thick trunk with pale-green rubbery leaves. In the spring, if it has received the proper light during the winter, it will flower with the most beautiful pink or white starry clusters. If you have any doubts as to your own light conditions, put it under a plant light and wait for the spring—it will be well worth it.

People who say that the jade plant never flowers indoors are wrong. It's just that it needs sixteen to eighteen hours of light to form buds. As the sun has the habit of setting each evening, you will have to supplement its rays with a plant light (unless, of course, you live in the Arctic).

Being a succulent, it stores water in its leaves. If the leaves start looking wrinkled, you haven't been watering enough. Luckily, this plant is like a camel and can take in large amounts of water, which keeps it going until the next drink. This ability to conserve water comes in very handy for propagation purposes.

Tip cuttings

Take off a four-inch tip cutting and set it aside for three days so that a callus will form over the cut.

Make up a soil mixture consisting of half potting soil and half sand (the sand makes the soil more porous). Crock the pot and fill it with the soil mixture. Press it down firmly. Make a hole with a stick for your cutting to go into. Press the soil around the stem to hold it firmly. Water the cutting with a vitamin B_1 solution.

Four-inch tip cutting

It is a good idea to put three or four cuttings together in a shallow pot. If you pinch them back and prune artistically, you get the effect of a miniature forest. Water once a week unless they start looking wrinkled—in which case, water twice a week.

Four cuttings root together.

70

KALANCHOE   *(Kalanchoe)*   Stonecrop Family

Kalanchoe, a succulent, is a member of the same family as echeveria and sedum, which gives you an idea of its likes and dislikes. Overwatering and poor light are its chief enemies—something I learned to my dismay after buying a very expensive and unusual plant only to have it lose all its lower leaves and do a slow droop. Luckily, I was able to save it by cutting it right back; this gave me a lot of cuttings, but the original plant was never quite the same again.

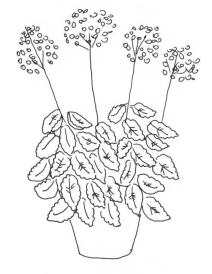

Kalanchoe blossfeldiana is a very popular plant that blooms in the winter with red or pink flowers. It can easily be propagated by taking tip cuttings. Root these in a sandy soil of half sand and half potting soil. Put five or six tip cuttings together in a shallow pot, and they will produce a nice, full plant. They can stay in the same sandy soil they are rooted in.

All succulents can be rooted from single leaves placed stalk down in moist sand. Put three or four into a shallow pot, cover it with plastic wrap and set it on the yogurt maker. New plantlets will form at the soil level; when these have at least two leaves, they can be lifted up and planted in their own pots. They like a good sandy soil (half sand and half soil), as they need good drainage.

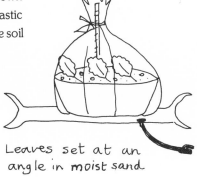

Leaves set at an angle in moist sand

K. pinnata is called "air plant" because it forms plantlets along the edges of its leaf. A single leaf, when planted in moist sand, will sprout three or four plantlets in the notches along the leaf edge.

A rarer version of a viviparous plant is *K. daigremontiana,* which grows up to forty plantlets along its leaf edges. This isn't as hard to grow as it is to pronounce. Place a leaf on moist soil, cover the pot with plastic wrap and set it on the yogurt maker. The little plantlets will slowly root in the sand and can be lifted up with a blunt pair of tweezers and placed in pots of their own. You will need a magnifying glass, as they are very small.

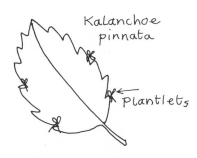

Kalanchoe pinnata

Plantlets

MAIDENHAIR FERN

(Adiantum cuneatum)

Fern Family

The maidenhair fern is one of the prettiest ferns to be found. Its very fragile dark stems are topped with wedge-shaped ruffly leaflets. Its problem, like that of so many of its cousins, is that after looking perfectly well one week, it will start turning brown and its leaves will dry up. This is caused by lack of humidity, so you should mist your plant daily and even put it into the shower stall from time to time after you have showered.

However, if this is information after the fact, cut back your plant to three or four inches of growth and let it start growing again.

Adiantum cuneatum

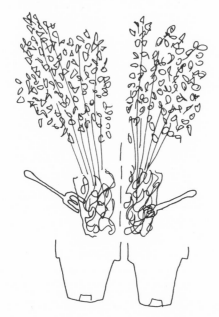

Division

On the other hand, if your fern is doing so well that it is climbing out of its pot, you will have to divide it. This is best done during the winter just before the new spring growth appears. Knock your plant gently out of its pot and pry the matted roots apart with two forks. Don't pull them apart completely or they will break; complete the division with a knife. Pot each section in its own pot in new soil and water it well.

It wouldn't be a bad idea to put both sections into plastic-bag greenhouses for a few days so that they will not wilt. But don't forget to harden them up before removing them from the humidity.

Always try to divide a plant during the winter, its dormant period. During the winter, most ferns stop producing new fronds; by dividing your plants at this time, you are not interfering with its natural functions. In other words, the plant will not have to divert its leaf-producing energy to heal its cut roots.

72

PEPEROMIA   *(Peperomia)*   ## Pepper Family

Many species and varieties of peperomia are good houseplants, and one provides us with our table pepper. Peperomias originally came from tropical South America, but they do not require the frequent watering and misting of most tropical plants. Because their roots do not grow deep, they do better in small shallow pots, allowing for overcrowding.

Peperomia griseo-argentea

Peperomias can easily be propagated by tip cuttings, which root in water or vermiculite. When the roots are one inch long, pot in soil. You can also root single leaves, like the African violet.

P. obtusifolia variegata

P. verschaffeltii

Water   Vermiculite

Leaves placed at an angle

Potted in soil

New plantlets form at base of leaf.

"Cake-pan" pot

Remove single firm leaves, each with about one inch of stem. Make up a "cake-pan" pot by inserting a small clay pot filled with water into a large bulb pot filled with vermiculite. Because the clay pot is porous, moisture will seep through its sides into the vermiculite, keeping it constantly moist. If you cannot find a cork to fit the hole in the small pot, use well-chewed chewing gum.

Place the single leaves around the vermiculite at an angle of 45 degrees. Warmth and humidity will help your leaves root, so put the pot into a plastic-bag greenhouse and set it on the yogurt maker.

New plantlets will form at the base of the parent leaf. When two or more leaves are visible, they can be carefully lifted from the vermiculite and planted in small individual pots of soil. Plant them at an angle, as shown in the drawing, so that the large leaf does not block their light.

PHILODENDRON

(Philodendron)

Arum or Calla Family

The arum (or calla) family seems to contain all our favorite houseplants: Chinese evergreen, caladium, anthurium, dieffenbachia, spathiphyllum and pothos. And the philodendron branch of the family has almost as many members itself.

Philodendrons can be classified as climbers and self-headers. They can further be divided into solid-leaved and cut-leaved plants.

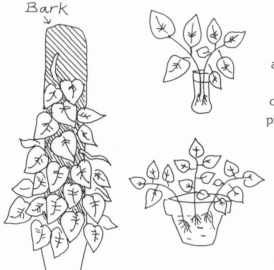

Bark

PHILODENDRON CORDATUM

Philodendron cordatum is a solid-leaved climber, and it is known also as an ivy type of philodendron. Its heart-shaped leaves grow and grow, clinging onto anything they can. They are often trained up a piece of moss-covered bark.

P. cordatum is very easy to propagate; as it grows like a weed in water, some people never bother to pot it at all! However, if you prefer to grow it in soil, wait for the roots to reach an inch in water, then pot two or three cuttings together in potting soil. Keep pinching it back or it will get very spindly on a thin stem.

P. HASTATUM RUBRUM 'RED DUCHESS'

This is a beautiful large-growing philodendron with arrow-shaped green leaves with a red tint to them, veined in red with a red underside. In rare circumstances *P. hastatum rubrum* will flower, but it is mainly grown for its beautiful leaves that can grow up to eighteen inches long. It is a solid-leaved climber and is usually trained to grow on a moss-covered piece of bark.

Nature has made it very easy to propagate this plant by providing the aerial roots that the plant uses to secure itself to its surroundings. Cut off a piece of the main stem just below such roots (which form at a node), and root it in water. New roots will grow in addition to the aerial roots already there. When these are two inches long, pot the cutting in soil. Put it into a plastic bag for a few days to recover from wilting and water it with the antishock mixture, a solution of vitamin B_1.

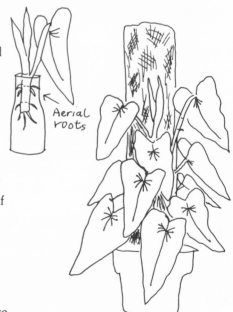

Aerial roots

74

P. WENDLANDII AND P. SELLOUM

P. wendlandii is a "self-heading" philodendron, and its brother *P. selloum* is a "cut-leaved self-header." They both grow from a single crown at the soil level. Plants growing this way often put out offsets at the soil level, and these can be rooted to form a new plant.

Take a sharp knife and cut off the offset as close to soil level as you can. If your plant is not too large, knock it out of its pot and trace the offset below the soil level where it joins the mother plant. Cut off a piece of the mother's roots with the offset to give it a good head start.

Plant the offset in a pot of vermiculite deep enough to hold the root without squashing it. Cover the pot with a plastic bag and set it on the yogurt maker for about a month. Don't forget to harden it up after taking it off the yogurt maker. Repot the little plant in soil—and you have a new plant.

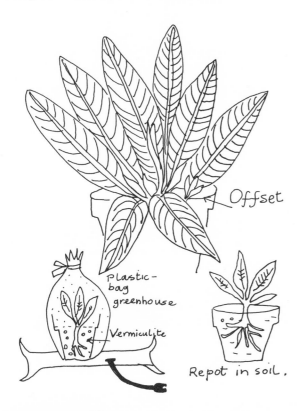

Offset

Plastic-bag greenhouse

Vermiculite

Repot in soil.

P. PERTUSUM

This split-leaf philodendron also goes by the name *Monstera deliciosa,* which means "delicious monster"—an indication that it produces a cucumberlike fruit which I believe is singularly unpleasant to the taste, if not downright poisonous. This is a cut-leaf climber and it grows best trained on a moss-covered board. As with all philodendrons that put out aerial roots, it is possible to propagate it by cutting off a piece of the stem.

Cut the stem just below the node where the aerial roots are. New roots will form in water; when they are an inch long, the plant can be potted in potting soil. Be careful to guard against wilting by putting the cutting into a plastic-bag greenhouse and watering it for a week with a solution of vitamin B_1 as an antishock treatment.

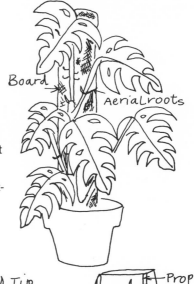

Board

Aerial roots

Tip cutting

Prop

Inverted plastic-bag greenhouse

75

PIGGYBACK PLANT

Saxifrage Family

(Tolmiea menziesii)

This wonderful little plant is a native of the northern California coast and can be found growing wild all the way up to Alaska. It was named after a Dr. Tolmie who was a surgeon with the Hudson's Bay Company. Its furry green leaves grow on top of one another—hence the nickname. The new leaves are of a paler green than the older leaves, giving the plant a light and dark effect which is very pretty.

This plant is *viviparous,* which freely translates to mean that new plants form directly on the leaves of the mother plant without the aid of seeds. It is such a slow grower that a mature plant is quite expensive. However, it is very easy to propagate.

Rooting in vermiculite

Stand the mother plant on a flat surface big enough to hold several small pots of vermiculite placed around her. Put a single clump of leaves into each pot, burying the bottom leaf, and secure the clump with a hairpin. Leave the clumps attached to the mother plant for at least a month, until roots have formed under the lower leaf.

Once the roots have formed, you can cut the umbilical cord. Empty out the vermiculite in each pot and repot each plantlet with potting soil.

There are two things to look out for when rooting your leaves this way: the vermiculite must be kept constantly moist, and the bottom leaf must be *under* the vermiculite or the roots will not form.

This seems a very complicated way of doing things because it is also easy to propagate your piggyback plant in water.

Back view showing roots forming under leaf

76

Rooting in water

Break off a clump of leaves and put it into a shallow glass dish of water, making sure that the bottom leaf is completely submerged. The roots will form only if the bottom leaf is *completely under the water.*

New roots will form in about one month in poor light, or in one week in good light. It makes a difference! To help the roots form, put the shallow dish into a small plastic bag, leaving the top of the bag open. This creates a small greenhouse and gives the leaf additional humidity.

When roots have formed, you can pot the plantlet in soil. Be sure that the bottom leaf is under the soil; bury it as an anchor to hold the plant in the pot.

This is one of those plants that give you a terrible time when you transfer it from water to soil. First of all, water it with a solution of vitamin B_1 as an antishock treatment. Then put it into a plastic-bag greenhouse for at least a week. Harden it up very, very slowly; take over three days as otherwise it will wilt again.

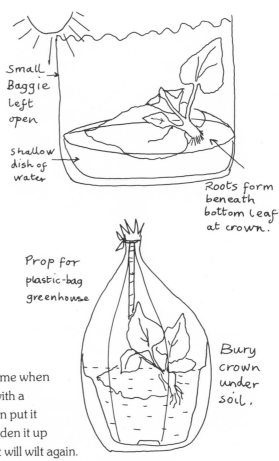

Small Baggie left open

shallow dish of water

Roots form beneath bottom leaf at crown.

Prop for plastic-bag greenhouse

Bury crown under soil.

Piggyback plants require, above all, good light. The minute the light level gets too dim, the leaves will crinkle up and die. They also seem to do well for a few months and then go into a mysterious decline. I think they suffer from plastic pots, so I always transfer them to clay pots at the first sign of drooping. They like to be well watered, but I don't believe they get enough oxygen in the nonporous plastic pots. I have taken my piggybacks out of their plastic pots and found a thin green line of algae on the interior of the pot—a sure sign that they are not getting enough oxygen. I also think that our houses are too warm for them because I've brought them back from death's door by cutting them right back and putting them outside for the summer, where they benefit from the cooler night temperatures.

They get attacked by mealybugs with hideous regularity. A good way to treat this is to swab them with a Q-tip dipped in alcohol.

As you see, they are very fussy, but well worth it.

Vodka 100 proof

White fluff like cotton? It's a mealy-bug.

PINEAPPLE *(Ananas comosus)* Pineapple Family

The pineapple is a bromeliad, one of those plants which perch on trees in the forest and which, having shallow roots, obtain most of their nutrients from the tropical rain. This is something to remember when growing a pineapple, as the only way it can be fed is by spraying it regularly with a very weak fertilizer.

Rooting the crown

When buying a pineapple to eat, pull at the leaves in the crown. If one comes away easily, that means that the pineapple is ripe and ready to eat. When you get it home, cut off the crown with two inches of the fruit attached. Put it aside to dry out for at least twenty-four hours. At the end of that time it will have developed a callus that will prevent it from losing any more moisture.

Crock a wide, shallow pot. Make up a mixture of three-quarters soil and one-quarter sand with a handful of peat moss thrown in for acidity. Plant the crown well down in the pot so that the two inches of fruit are completely covered with soil. Water it and spray the crown with a mixture of your usual fertilizer made one-eighth as strong as normal. Spray with this mixture twice a week and mist at least once a day with plain water. If the soil appears to be very dry, carefully add a little water around the sides of the pot, but not directly onto the crown under the soil or it may rot.

Crown
2 inches

Your plant will grow very slowly, looking just like its bromeliad cousins. But whereas bromeliads develop beautiful flowers, it is most unusual for a pineapple to flower indoors. However, it puts out strong suckers at its base which are called "ratoons," and these give the plant a more interesting shape. If your plant develops more than one sucker, why not start a completely new plant? The sucker grows up from below the surface of the soil, so cut it off with its roots intact and plant it in the same soil mixture as its mother.

Sucker
soil level

Although I said that homegrown pineapples do not usually flower and bear fruit, this miracle has been known to happen when the plant is grown under a plant light.

And then you can start the whole process again!

78

POINSETTIA   *(Euphorbia pulcherrima)*   Spurge Family

The beloved poinsettia with its beautiful red flowering heads has recently been tamed to pot size, and in the last couple of years a miniature version has been produced. It is the most glorious plant to receive in the midst of the winter, and it lights up any room. After a few weeks, gradually one leaf, then another, falls off, until you are finally left with a very straggly-looking plant which you usually throw out. But this year, after reading my book, you will know better; you will hang onto the plant, nursing it back to glory for next Christmas and making cuttings from it at the same time.

After the red leaves (bracts) have dropped, three or four spindly stems will be left. Cut them back to six inches and put them somewhere out of public view, as they don't look particularly beautiful. Continue to water them, but gradually cut down the water until you are giving them a scant cup per week. This is their dormant period, so you won't see much growth until spring. However, as soon as you see new shoots appearing, put the plant back in good light and start watering regularly.

What starts out in glory

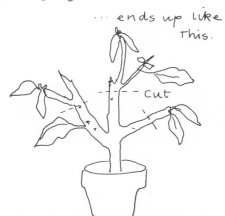

... ends up like this.

cut

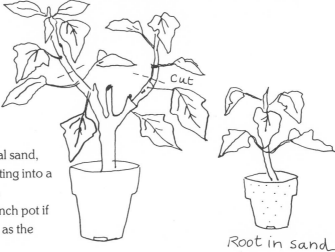

New growth

Cut

Root in sand.

Stem cutting

By early summer the stems will have put out new leaves and branches, and it is those new branches that become your cuttings. Cut off a stem just below the third node.

Crock a pot and fill it with horticultural sand, which is heavy and rough. Put each cutting into a small pot. A three-inch pot is good for a normal-sized poinsettia, but use a two-inch pot if you are cutting back a dwarf poinsettia, as the stems are much narrower and shorter.

Light requirements

Give your cuttings the best light in the house—even a plant light. Cover them with jam jars or put them into greenhouses of plastic bags, as they need humidity to root. A short period on the yogurt maker also helps.

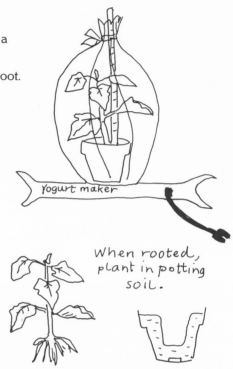

yogurt maker

When rooted, plant in potting soil.

After one month, give your cuttings a gentle tug. If you feel a resistance, it means that roots have formed. Carefully lift each cutting out of the sand, pour the sand out and keep for future use, then pot the cutting in soil in the same pot. Poinsettias need very bright light in order to produce flowers, so you should put them under a plant light.

Which brings us to another problem. For poinsettias to flower, they must have at least fifteen hours of darkness (corresponding to winter sunrise and sunset) for a period of four to six weeks. So if you want color for Christmas, you had better start planning around mid-November. If you are a very well-regulated person with a good memory, all you have to do is take them from the light at 5 P.M. each day and put them into a pitch-black cupboard (where they won't see a glimmer of light) until 8 A.M. the next day. If, however, you are like me, very disorganized and with a memory that's not too marvelous either, you had better make other arrangements.

The best solution I have found is to put the cuttings into an unused cupboard on November 15 with a plant light and an automatic timer set to go on at 8 A.M. and off at 5 P.M. I look in at them every day to water and fertilize them. By mid-December the tight knots that herald the arrival of the red bracts appear, much to my relief. Then I take the cuttings out of the cupboard and put them somewhere where they can be appreciated.

All this messing about with lights is a dreadful nuisance, but unfortunately it is necessary if you want your plants to flower for Christmas. I have often wondered how it is that the poinsettia trees on our street bloom regularly for Christmas without going through all this trouble. After all, no one turns off the street lights for them during their brooding season. It's one of nature's puzzles.

For a very good way to plant poinsettias in a basket, *see page 114.*

POLKA-DOT PLANT   Acanthus Family
(Hypoestes sanguinolenta)

This plant is also known as the "German-measles" plant because of the pink spots on its leaves. These markings show up better when the plant is in good light. This plant is such a rapid grower that it resembles a weed—which it probably is in its normal jungle habitat. It can grow in pots, planters and baskets, but it *must* be pinched back very often in its formative stage or it will grow three feet long on a single stem.

Pinch back here at tips.

I speak from experience because I have a friend who refused to pinch it back. He insisted that the plant knew what it was doing, and he didn't want to interfere with nature. Three weeks later he called again and said that it was growing so tall that it had fallen over. I told him to cut it back to six inches and to cut the stems into pieces which he could root in water. That's what he *should* have done because at last count the plant was five feet tall and so spindly that he had stapled it to the wall—which is not necessarily the best treatment for a plant.

What you must remember is that *a plant that grows like a weed must be pruned with enthusiasm.* Once your plant's stems show more than three sets of leaves, you can pinch them back.

Tip cutting

You can also leave it until it has six sets of leaves and make a tip cutting of three sets of leaves and root it in water. This regular pruning will force your plant to branch out at the soil level and produce a nice bushy plant.

Once the roots are an inch long, you can pot the stems in potting soil. Take a four-inch pot and put three or four stems into the soil together. Cover the pot with a plastic-bag greenhouse for a few days and water it with a solution of vitamin B_1 as an antishock treatment for the first week. Don't forget to harden up your plant before removing it from its greenhouse.

The polka-dot plant will lose its polka dots if the light is too dim. I have mine growing on a bright windowsill, and it is doing so well that it has produced pretty pale purple spikes of flowers.

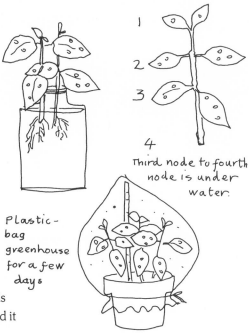

1
2
3
4
Third node to fourth node is under water.

Plastic-bag greenhouse for a few days

PRAYER PLANT   *(Maranta)*   Arrowroot Family

This is a truly charming plant with a unique habit: at night it folds up its leaves and says its prayers—hence its name. Its leaves glow with the colors of a peacock, and its natural habitat is the floor of the rain forests. So remember to mist it regularly and grow it where the sun does not shine directly onto its delicate leaves.

Maranta arundinacea is the source of kitchen arrowroot. The maranta that is generally grown for the house is *M. leuconeura massangeana* (meaning white-veined). In Brazil, where it grows with greeny-brown markings, it is called the "rabbit-track plant."

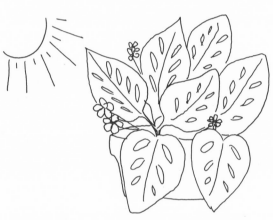

Cuttings can be taken at any time and will root quickly in water in a bright light. When roots are one inch long, pot the cuttings in soil. Water with a vitamin B_1 solution as an antishock treatment and cover with a plastic bag for a few days to overcome any wilting.

When the plant grows large, it is possible to divide it. This should be done in the winter while it is in a semidormant state. Knock the plant out of its pot and pry the roots apart with two forks. Cut the roots into two sections and pot each section in pots one size smaller than the original pot.

In England this shy and unassuming plant is called "husband and wife." I can't imagine why, unless it's because, like all good married couples, they say their prayers together before going to sleep.

82

RABBIT'S-FOOT FERN   Fern Family

(Davallia trichomanioides canariensis)

This delicate little fern, which comes from the Old World, is also called "bear's-foot" or "squirrel's-foot" fern. Confusingly, a larger, coarser relative, *(Polypodium aureum)* is also known as "hare's-foot" or "bear's-foot" fern. However, it really doesn't matter for our purposes, since they are both propagated in exactly the same way. Both grow from creeping rhizomes which grow upon, rather than under, the surface of the soil.

My neighbor Polly, who has some very unusual plants, gave me my first cuttings from her plant, which had grown so large that the hairy rhizomes had completely covered the basket it was planted in. Because of this climbing characteristic, this fern looks best in a wire basket.

Making a hanging basket

Get a round basket if you want it to hang free or a "half-circle" basket if you want to hang it against a wall. You will also need sphagnum moss, pieces of picture wire, potting soil, a plastic bag and ten cuttings, each piece three inches long.

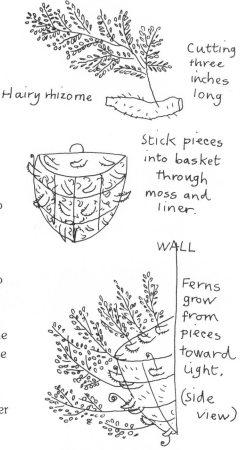

Hairy rhizome

Cutting three inches long

Stick pieces into basket through moss and liner.

WALL

Ferns grow from pieces toward light. (side view)

Soak the sphagnum moss in water and wring it out. Line the basket with the moss and use the picture wire to secure it to the basket in one or two places. Put two inches of soil into the plastic bag and insert it into the basket on top of the moss. This will be used as a liner to prevent the moss and soil from drying out too quickly, so trim the top of the bag down to the top of the basket.

Starting near the bottom, poke a hole through both the moss and the plastic bag with a screwdriver. Insert a piece of rhizome into the hole and press the soil around it. Continue inserting the rhizomes, working from the bottom up in layers. As you insert each layer, add another two inches of soil to cover it and hold it in place.

When you have finished inserting all your pieces, you will have a strange-looking basket with pieces of hairy roots sticking out. Don't worry about looks because within a year you will have the most beautiful lacy, delicate fiddleheads, which will unravel and become ferns. Very soon the entire basket will be covered with a curtain of beautiful fronds. The rhizomes will continue to grow across the surface of the basket, and you can cut pieces off if you want to start another basket or fill in any gaps. Mist the ferns regularly and keep the soil moist.

83

RICE-PAPER PLANT *(Fatsia japonica)* Ginseng Family

The fatsia is a lovely plant whose glossy green leaves have between five and nine lobes, like fingers. It grows up on a central stem; as it gets older, offsets form at its feet which can be cut off to form new plants. The fatsia is a fast grower, particularly in the spring when it puts out a great burst of growth, forming new crowns on top of the previous leaves. When it is grown in bright light, large airy white flowers form, and they in turn become clusters of black berries.

I learned about the propagation of fatsias by accident after I left my plant outside to get some sun.

We have a gardener of whom one can only charitably say that he would be better suited in another profession—butcher. He came along with his karate shears, pruning in his overdedicated way, and cut off the entire one-foot crown of spring growth. I didn't notice its loss until a few hours later, but luckily I was able to rescue the crown from the dustbin, a little squashed but none the worse.

It was cut here.

Offsets

Crown cutting

Now here was a case of "yogurt maker to the rescue," as I don't think it could have survived without bottom heat to help it root. I trimmed off the outside leaves from the crown, leaving just the smaller inside cluster. I filled a deep pot with three-quarters potting soil and one-quarter sand and buried the crown halfway down with just the top part of the crown and the central leaves above the surface. I stuck in two bamboo sticks and over them slipped the long plastic envelope our daily newspaper comes in on rainy days. Then I watered the crown with a vitamin B_1 solution to help it recover from the shock and to stimulate root production.

I set it on the yogurt maker under the plant lamp, which I left on all night to give it strength. After three hours a mist formed on the inside of the plastic, which indicated that the greenhouse was working.

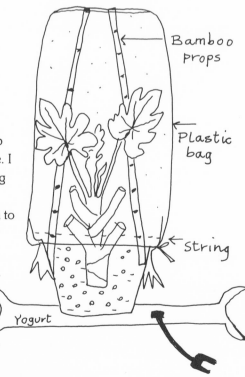

Bamboo props

Plastic bag

String

Yogurt

The leaves recovered from the shock, straightened up and even started growing. I wish I could tell you the end of the story, but all this happened only a month ago.

In my experience a plant that was not going to survive would have already died. Its leaves would have continued to wilt, and nothing would have saved it. But as everything looks good under the plastic cover, I shall leave it there for six weeks. The soil seems a little dry, but as there is still a mist on the plastic bag, I don't want to add any more or the crown might rot.

After six weeks I will take the pot off the yogurt maker and slowly harden it up. Then I will put it into a bright window, fertilize it and introduce it to the other plants. I am glad to say that my original fatsia suffered no ill effects after being decapitated; in fact, it has started to put out some new offsets at its base. Obviously decapitation is a rather severe form of pinching back!

FATSHEDERA LIZEI

This genetic wonder is a cross between the fatsia and the English ivy *(Hedera helix)*. Its leaves have fewer fingers than the fatsia—only five lobes, making it look more like ivy. In fact, its common name is "tree ivy."

I helped myself to a small tip cutting when no one was looking and it rooted in water in only two weeks. It takes after the ivy part of the family because it grows in a helical form rather than in a crown like the fatsia.

After a month, when the roots were an inch long, I planted my cutting in soil and had a lovely new plant. I watered it with a vitamin B_1 solution to prevent wilting and was ready to put it into a greenhouse at the first sign, but it wasn't necessary.

It does very well with less light than the fatsia and is a very undemanding and lovely plant.

RUBBER PLANT   *(Ficus elastica decora)*   Fig Family

This is a wondrously even-tempered plant that regularly takes abuse without getting offended, so it's no wonder it is so popular. It originally grew in India and Malaya, but has been tamed to pot size. It is the standby of every indoor gardener and should be the first plant you ever buy because it is so rewarding. There are three ways to propagate this plant, which makes it an excellent lesson on methods of propagation.

Rooting in water

You have been given a small rubber plant and now, one year later, it has grown over two feet tall on a single spindly stem. Cut off the topknot with six to eight inches of stem. Stand it in a jar of water on a bright windowsill. Roots will form in four to six weeks, and the plant can be potted in soil. The mother plant will put out a side shoot just under the incision and in this way can be forced to branch out. You can repot the little plant in the same pot as its young mother.

Cut.

Prop up in narrow bottle of water.

Air layering

Your old and most beloved rubber plant has lost all its lower leaves, owing either to exhaustion or to overwatering. Now is the time to air layer it.

Make a cut three-quarters of the way through the stem at an angle of 45 degrees, just above where you want the new roots to form. Insert a toothpick into the cut to prevent it from sealing itself shut. Dust the cut with hormone powder. Take a handful of sphagnum moss, soak it in water and wring it out, and wrap it around the cut stem. Now cover the moss with plastic wrap and tie it at the top and bottom with Twist-ems.

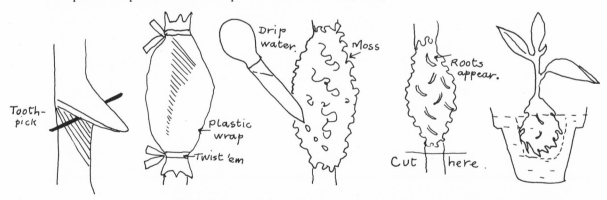

Tooth-pick   *Plastic wrap*   *Twist 'em*   *Drip water.*   *Moss*   *Roots appear.*   *Cut here.*

Check the moss frequently to make sure that it doesn't dry out and add water by dripping it from a household meat baster. Add some vitamin B_1 to the water as a root stimulant. When roots appear through the moss, remove the plastic wrap, cut the stem just below the roots, and plant the root ball in a pot of soil.

Stem cuttings

If you have air layered your plant, you are left with a large expanse of scarred stem, denuded of leaves. Instead of throwing away the plant at this stage, try stem propagation.

What you are trying to do is force an old gnarled stem into putting out new shoots (something it probably forgot about since those glorious days of youth).

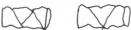

three-inch pieces

Cut the stem into three-inch pieces. Crock a shallow pot and fill it halfway with prepared vermiculite. Half bury the stems in the vermiculite.

Cover the pot with plastic wrap tied under the lip of the pot with string. Make one or two holes in the plastic so that a little air can circulate.

Set the pot on the yogurt maker, as it is just about impossible to make stem cuttings without bottom heat. Water with a vitamin B$_1$ solution to stimulate root production.

In six to eight weeks little green shoots will appear on the stems, and these are the new plants. When the shoots are one inch tall, remove the pot from the yogurt maker and slowly harden it up.

Harden up when shoots are one inch tall.

Crock a four-inch pot for each of the stem cuttings. Carefully lift the stems out of the vermiculite and plant each one in potting soil. Bury the stems completely in the soil, with just the green shoots showing above the surface. Water with the vitamin B$_1$ as an antishock treatment.

Bury stem in potting soil with shoots above surface.

Original plant with new shoot

Wait! Don't throw away your original plant because you're not finished yet. Quite often, if you continue caring for your plant, a new shoot will appear just below the stub. I have noticed a strange thing: it takes the exact length of time—about two months—for the roots to appear in air layering, for the shoot to appear in stem cuttings and for the new shoot to appear on your original plant. Mother Nature has built a very precise time clock into her plants, and there's no hurrying her up.

SCREW PINE   *(Pandanus veitchii)*   Screw-Pine Family

This is one of Mother Nature's miraculously geometric plants, whose leaves grow in a perfect spiral up its stem. It is charming as a young plant, but as it grows older, its serrated leaves have a way of turning into teeth that give you a good nip whenever you try to dodge them to water the plant.

Pandanus veitchii has green-and-white-striped leaves and seems to be more popular than its yellow-and-brown-striped cousin, *P. sanderi*.

The mature plant puts out offsets in the form of suckers which are attached to the mother plant below the soil level. These can be removed to form a new plant.

When dealing with a mature screw pine, you would be well advised to wear strong gloves and even to wrap the head of the plant in a pillowcase so it won't get at you while you are working on it.

Gently knock the plant out of its pot and find the place where the sucker is joined to the mother. Take a sharp knife and cut downward, severing a portion of the mother's roots with the sucker.

The size of the pot you choose will depend upon how much of the mother's roots you took. There must be enough depth in the pot for the root to lie without being squashed or bent.

Crock the pot and fill it with potting soil. Make a hole in the center of the soil large enough to hold the root. Push the root in gently and press the soil around it firmly. Bang the pot to settle the soil.

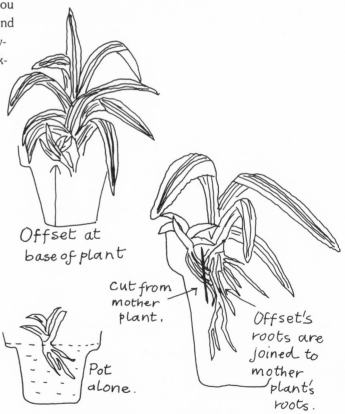

Offset at base of plant

Cut from mother plant.

Pot alone.

Offset's roots are joined to mother plant's roots.

88

You may have trouble knocking your plant out of its pot. One knock too many and you're going to have more crocks. If, after a couple of soft knocks, the plant doesn't slide out of its pot smoothly, you will have to reconsider the matter.

You can cut off the offset at the soil level. However, as you can imagine, this makes it harder for the new plant to adjust; it has to grow roots of its own, so it should be treated differently.

Take your sharp knife and cut the offset away from the mother plant as low as you can. Prepare a three-inch pot with vermiculite and press the offset into the moist surface. Cover the pot with a jam jar and set it on the yogurt maker.

Press the offset into the moist vermiculite. Cover with jam jar.

I have been taking it for granted that you have a yogurt maker. In case you don't have one, there are a couple of other things you can do.

If you are making the cutting in winter and you have a radiator that provides a source of constant heat, this will do just as well. Don't set the pot directly on the radiator, however, as it might be too hot.

It would be better to fill a cake pan with pebbles and put the pot onto the pebbles. Fill the cake pan with water and test it with your finger after two or three hours. If the water seems very hot, the radiator won't do, although it's unlikely that it would get any hotter than lukewarm.

The space over the pilot light on a gas stove would be ideal if you never cooked, but as the bottom heat has to be constant, you would ruin the effect by having to move the plant every time you made coffee.

SEEDS
GRAPES

(Vitis)

GRAPE FAMILY

I really prefer seedless grapes but, as you know, seeds are needed to grow new plants.

Wash off a handful of grape seeds and dry them with a paper towel. As with citrus seeds, soaking them overnight helps soften them up and hastens germination.

Because grape seeds are so much smaller than citrus seeds, it is easier to plant a handful of them in the same pot, hoping that at least some of them will germinate. Leave some space between each seed, or you will have difficulty separating their roots. As each seedling pokes its head through the soil, you can "prick it out," which means transplant it to its own four- to six-inch pot. (See page 107.)

Grapes grow on vines, and vines like to climb, so be prepared to provide your vine with a support. To begin with, a narrow stake with one or two crossbars will be sufficient. If your vine grows very big, you may have to get a trellis.

Grapevines go through seasonal changes of color, turning red in autumn and even dropping their leaves. If this happens, do not worry.

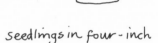

Seed leaves appear.

Grapevines should be cut back each winter so that they are no more than twelve inches tall. This forces the plant into semidormancy. Moderate the watering while your plant rests during the winter, but give it enough so that the soil doesn't dry out completely.

seedlings in four-inch pots

As soon as you see new growth appearing, spring is on the way. Go back to watering and fertilizing your vine regularly. I don't make any promises about having luscious grapes from your vines; but its leaves are so pretty that I am sure you won't feel cheated.

Cut back in winter to twelve inches.

Cut back to last year's old wood. New branches form in the spring.

Two-year-old vine

90

SEEDS

LEMON, ORANGE AND GRAPEFRUIT   *(Citrus)*   **CITRUS FAMILY**

Sometime you may be lucky when cutting open a grapefruit and discover a seed that has already begun sprouting. In this case, all you have to do is plant the sprouted seed directly in soil. It will grow into a grapefruit tree.

But mostly you will find that citrus fruit seeds have not sprouted, so you will have to coax them into germination yourself.

Soak the seeds in water overnight and place them on paper towels to dry. Find a shallow glass or plastic container with a tight-fitting lid and line it with two or three layers of sterile gauze, wetting them thoroughly and draining off any excess water.

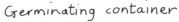

Germinating container

Lay the seeds on the gauze, close up the container and put it into a dark place. Most seeds need darkness to germinate. Take a peek from day to day until the seeds open and the first leaves appear. These are the cotyledons, the seed leaves; the second pair of leaves, the true leaves, will follow shortly.

As soon as the second set of leaves is one to two inches tall, you can plant the seed.

Crock a small three- to four-inch pot and fill it with a mixture of three-quarters potting soil and one-quarter sand. With a pencil make a hole for the tiny plant and, carefully lifting it by its seed leaves, place it in its hole. The second set of leaves should lie just above soil level.

Be sure that you never allow your plant to dry out, as citrus seeds need regular watering. Put it into your sunniest window or under a plant light. It is very doubtful that your citrus tree will bear fruit; but, as it is such a charming guest to have staying in your house, appreciate it for its good looks and the fact that you grew it yourself from seed.

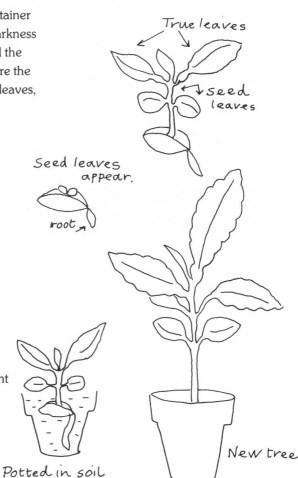

True leaves

seed leaves

Seed leaves appear.

root

Potted in soil

New tree

SNAKE PLANT   (Sansevieria)   Lily Family

This plant is also called "mother-in-law's tongue," which insults either your mother-in-law or your plant, depending upon whom you prefer. It is one of those plants that have taken years of abuse and neglect like the humble aspidistra, both of which you see relegated to the backgrounds of Victorian prints.

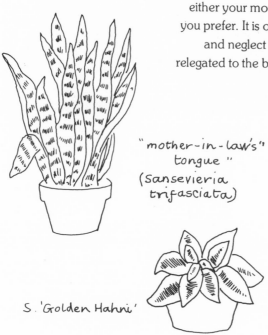

"mother-in-law's" tongue " (Sansevieria trifasciata)

S. 'Golden Hahni'

There are two general types of sansevieria: the tall type *(Sansevieria trifasciata)* with sword-shaped leaves that twist around one another and grow upright to five feet tall; and a bird's-nest type that grows in a low rosette. Mr. Hahn (of miniature-ivy fame) has produced this new rosette type of sansevieria, which is called a "sport," a name given to offspring that has different characteristics from its forebears. Whereas among humans such a child might be regarded with mixed emotions and a few raised eyebrows, in horticulture it is a cause for great rejoicing and is welcomed with open arms. Mr. Hahn's sport, 'Golden Hahni,' has two golden bands running up each leaf.

Leaf cuttings

With *Sansevieria trifasciata,* cut a long leaf from the parent plant and divide it into pieces four inches long. It is important to remember which is the top edge of the leaf, and it is a good idea to make a small notch on this edge, because the leaf will form roots only from its bottom edge. Lay your sections aside for two days so a callus will form.

With *S.* 'Golden Hahni,' cut a single leaf straight along its bottom edge. If you want several plants, cut several leaves.

In making leaf cuttings of both plants, crock a shallow pot and fill it with sand. Water it well with a vitamin B_1 solution and put in your pieces of leaf in an upright position, half-buried in the sand.

Leaf cuttings require both humidity and bottom heat to produce roots. Put the pot into a plastic bag and set it on the yogurt maker. Be sure to give it good light.

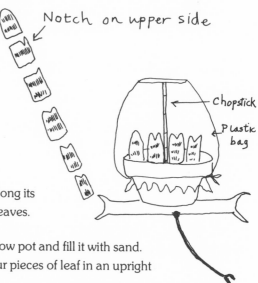

Notch on upper side

Chopstick

Plastic bag

92

Propagation by Offsets

All rosette-type sansevierias put out offsets at the soil level and can be propagated this way.

With a sharp knife, cut the offset from the parent plant. Crock a small pot with sand and water it with a vitamin B₁ solution. Press the offset into the sand, cover it with a jam jar and set it on the yogurt maker.

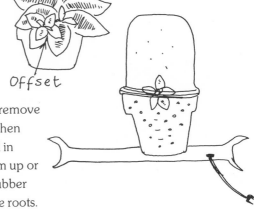

Offset

When the roots have formed, in a month to six weeks, remove them from the yogurt maker, harden them up gradually, then pot them in a mixture of half soil and half sand. Be careful in lifting them out of the rooting medium; don't just pull them up or the roots will break off. Dig them out from below with a rubber spatula, taking some of the rooting medium along with the roots.

Division

If your sansevieria is the type that has variegated green-and-yellow-striped leaves, you will find that leaf cuttings grown from its leaves create a solid green offspring. The only way to get a striped copy, in this instance, is to divide it.

Knock your plant out of its pot and shake off as much soil as you can so that you can see the roots clearly. Try to pry the roots apart with a couple of forks. This is simply horrible to do because you feel as if you are mutilating your plant.

You can divide it into as many sections as you want, but make sure that each section of the root has a few leaves. If you have made four sections from one plant, put them into small pots. If you have divided your plant into two sections, the new pots can be just a little smaller than the original.

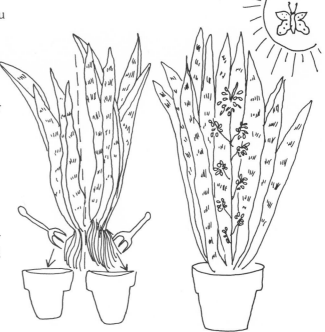

Sansevierias are commonly grown in very poor light and have the reputation of being "low light-requiring plants." This isn't necessarily true, as I once saw a sansevieria that was actually blooming! Its owner said that it was because he had put it into a sunny window. It had a beautiful spray of flowers that smelled like a tuberose. So take your long-suffering plant out of its dark corner, put it into your brightest window and see what happens.

SPATHIPHYLLUM　　Arum or Calla Family
(Spathiphyllum)

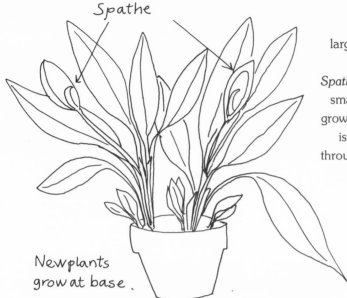

Spathe

This beautiful plant is a member of the largest family of houseplants, which includes philodendron, pothos and dieffenbachia. *Spathiphyllum floribundum* has leaves that are smaller than the *S. clevelandii,* whose leaves grow over a foot long. The beauty of this plant is that it puts out lilylike flowers from spring through summer.

New plants grow at base.

Mature plant grows from thick crown.

I read that this is a plant that does well in dim light, but I found that my plant wouldn't bloom at all until I put it into a sunny window and reinforced the light with a plant lamp. It is one of my favorite plants because it is so easy to please. As soon as it needs watering, the leaves begin to droop, and you can rescue it without worrying about overwatering.

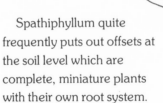

Offsets

Spathiphyllum quite frequently puts out offsets at the soil level which are complete, miniature plants with their own root system.

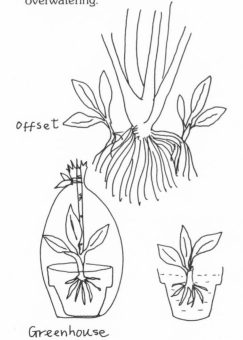

offset

Greenhouse

Knock your plant out of its pot and gently pull the offset away from its parent. Its roots will be connected to its mom and will have to be cut apart. Pot the little fellow in a three- to four-inch pot and put him into a plastic bag for a day or two in case he has difficulty adjusting to his new life. Water with a vitamin B_1 solution as an antishock treatment for the first week.

My large spathiphyllum is over five years old, and what was originally two smallish plants in one pot has become a mass of offsets with two enormous three-foot mature plants towering over them. It is time to divide it.

Division

Knock your plant out of its pot and brush off any loose soil. Lay your plant flat on a table and examine the rootstocks. You will notice that your one large plant is made up of smaller plants crowded around the main plant.

Divide the leaves into two sections and then pry the roots apart with your hands. Each section must have leaves, shoots of new growth and roots. Now cut the two sections apart with a sharp knife. For many years I avoided dividing my plants because I hated cutting their roots apart. But once I did it for the first time (and saw that I hadn't killed the plant), it wasn't quite so bad thereafter.

You can divide your plant into more than two sections if you want to. The sizes of the pots they go into depend upon how many sections you have. Unless you are prepared to cut off some of the roots at the bottom, a large plant cut into two sections will have to go back into a pot the same size that it just left. When divided into three or four sections, your pots should be six inches in diameter.

Spathiphyllum is a plant that grows thick white rootstocks which occasionally force the plant out of its pot. If your plant has begun to tilt and its crown is above the surface, you can be sure that it has become root-bound and needs to be put into a larger pot. (See page 113.)

Another sign that a plant is root-bound is that you have difficulty watering it. Either the water refuses to go down into the pot and stays on top, or conversely, it runs straight down the sides and out of the bottom hole.

Ice cubes are a convenient method of watering your plant if it is root-bound. The ice takes so long to melt that the roots have a chance to absorb it. However, sooner or later you are going to have to divide your plant or put it into a larger pot.

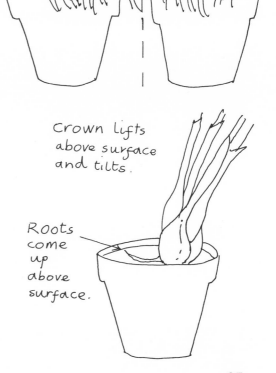

Divide into two.

Crown lifts above surface and tilts.

Roots come up above surface.

SPIDER PLANT   *(Chlorophytum elatum)*   Lily Family

My beloved spider plant is six years old and is of infinite fecundity, having provided my friends and *their* friends with baby spiders year in, year out.

This is the plant that starts off in a two-inch pot and each year gets repotted in increasingly larger pots until it becomes so big that it looks as if it will bring the roof down. There is nothing lovelier than hanging up a really large spider plant with space around it so that you can appreciate the curtain of plantlets.

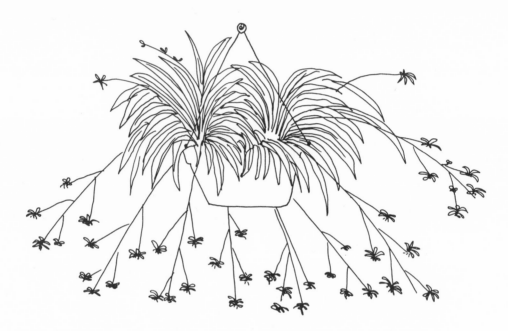

The spider plant is a very easy plant to propagate, but it grows very slowly for the first two years. As it gets larger, it seems to climb out of its pot, and this is an indication that it needs a larger pot. I always put three or four two-year-old plants into a big pot, which gives the effect of a much older and larger plant. In the spring the spider puts out runners on long stems, each runner having small white flowers and five or six plantlets growing at the end of small branching stems. As these grow older, they get heavier and hang down below the pot. This is your material for new plants.

Rooting in water

The young plantlet is attached to the runner at its roots and can be pulled off. Lay it in a small dish of water, making sure that its roots are always in the water. Top up the water level daily.

Roots

Roots grow longer in water.

96

Within a week thick white roots will appear. When they are two inches long, you can pot the plant in potting soil. I always put two or three together in a six-inch pot because one on its own seems so tiny. As it grows larger, it will fill up the pot; if it appears to be growing out over the side of the pot, that means that it is getting too large for its home.

Spider plants look very nice in a mixed planting with grape ivy and pothos.

Three plantlets in six-inch pot

←Crown

Roots grow longer.

Rooting in vermiculite

Another way to propagate this plant may be cowardly, but it resembles nature's own way of doing it. Pin down a plantlet in a pot of prepared vermiculite at the side of the mother plant. With this method you don't have to cut the umbilical cord until you are sure that the plantlet has rooted—giving you a built-in safety factor.

The only disadvantage to this method is that you can do it only if your mother plant is *not* hanging up. Your mother plant must be on a flat surface so that the small plantlets can be grouped around her. Use hairpins to secure the plantlets to the vermiculite, which must always be damp.

Pay attention to your spider plant when you water it. If the water seems to run straight out of the bottom hole, it is because the roots have taken up all the space in the pot and have pulled the remaining soil away from the sides. You can sometimes counteract this by forcing additional soil down the sides of the pot, pushing it down with a chopstick.

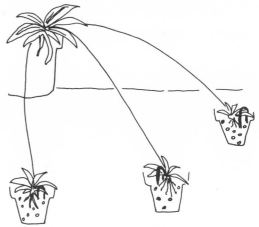

Hairpins hold the plantlets down in vermiculite.

You can also knock the plant out of its pot and cut off an inch of roots all around. It is rather merciless, but the plants always survive, Add new soil to the bottom of the pot and around the edges, pressing it into the spaces. Bang the pot on the ground a couple of times to settle the soil.

Spiders like good light but are inclined to bleach out if they get too much sunshine. Watch out for scale, which are small insects like brown ladybugs. Brush them off with a toothbrush dipped in vodka.

STAGHORN FERN *(Platycerium bifurcatum)* Fern Family

You have surely seen this fern growing on the wall like some great moose trophy; it is very much beloved by interior decorators for bachelor apártments. I can't say that this is my favorite fern, but it certainly has character. It is epiphytic, which means that in its native habitat, the tropics, it perches on trees. Dead vegetation collects around its roots to form a "nest."

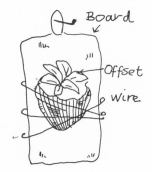

Indoors, staghorn ferns are usually mounted and grown against a large wooden wall plank. Their shallow roots are encased in sphagnum moss or osmunda fiber, which holds the soil in lieu of pots. Staghorns form offsets at the base of the mother plant, and these can be cut off with a sharp knife and grown in a "nest."

Making a nest for the offset

You will need a plank or a board, picture wire and the special soil used by epiphytic plants—very coarse and porous. An orchid nursery or a good garden supply shop should have the special soil. (For directions on making up this soil yourself, see page 31.) Finally, you will need sphagnum moss or osmunda fiber, which can be used interchangeably.

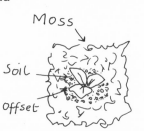

Soak the moss in water, wring it out and lay it flat. Put a handful of the special soil in the middle of the moss, then place the offset in the middle of the soil. Wrap the moss around the offset and its soil so that it forms a nest. Tie the picture wire around the nest to hold it together. Lay the board flat and wire the nest to the board, then hang it on a wall.

Any epiphytic plant presents a watering problem indoors because the water runs straight through the loosely packed nest. If it is a small staghorn, you can take it into the kitchen and water it in the sink. But if it is large, you will have a problem. You can slip a plastic bag under the plant and bring it up over the nest while watering, so that the runoff remains in the bottom of the bag. Mist it regularly to provide humidity.

Staghorn ferns can grow very large and seemingly forever. There is one at my nursery which is reputed to be at least twenty-five years old. It has grown so large that it regularly pulls itself loose from its overhead hook and requires the services of four grown men to hoist it back again.

STRAWBERRY GERANIUM   Saxifrage Family
(Saxifraga sarmentosa)

This is a strange name for a plant that is neither a strawberry nor a geranium, but it throws off runners like a strawberry and its leaves are shaped like a geranium. Its hairy leaves are dark olive-green with grayish marks on the upper sides and reddish marks on the undersides. Its tiny white flowers grow on tall stems. It puts out runners which hang below the pot; therefore, like its fellow plants that put out runners, the piggyback and spider plants, it looks best when hanging.

Propagation by runners

The easiest way to propagate this plant is to cut off a runner and let it form roots in a tiny bottle of water. When rooted, you can plant it in potting soil in a small pot. However, as the runners are so small, it might be easier to pin them down in a pot of vermiculite next to the mother plant. You will have to stand the mother plant on a flat surface and group the pots around her. Roots form in a month to six weeks, and the new plant can be potted in soil in the same pot.

Don't leave it attached to its mother any longer than necessary—apart from being a drain on the mother's food supply, there is a time for every plant to learn to face the world on its own.

Water

Pin runners down in a pot of vermiculite.

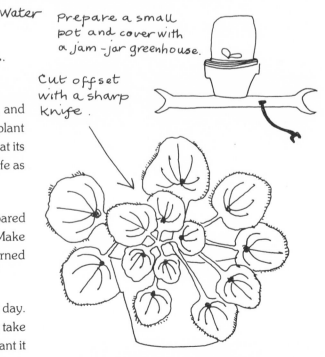

Prepare a small pot and cover with a jam-jar greenhouse.

Cut offset with a sharp knife.

Propagation by offsets

This plant grows from a central crown, and even in the smallest pot your one original plant will soon be joined by offsets which grow at its base. These can be cut off with a sharp knife as close as possible to the soil level.

Put the offset into a small pot of prepared vermiculite and set it on the yogurt maker. Make a greenhouse with a plastic bag or an upturned jam jar balanced on the rim of the pot.

Water with a vitamin B_1 solution the first day. After a month to six weeks, roots will form; take it off the yogurt maker and harden it up. Plant it in soil in the same pot.

Offset growing on top of mother plant

99

SUGARCANE

Grass Family

(Saccharum officinarum)

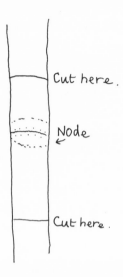

Cut here.

Node

Cut here.

It's hard to think of sugarcane as being alive—it looks just like bamboo as it stands around in bunches waiting for someone to take it home. But you can actually cut off a small piece of the stem and make a mallet cutting.

The stem is divided into sections, which give it that "bamboo look." At each dividing line, there is an incipient node with the off-chance that behind it a bud is lurking.

Fill a shallow pot with a soil mixture of half sand and half soil. Lay your piece of sugarcane horizontally on the surface of the soil and push it down until it is half-buried.

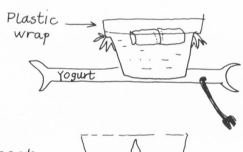

Plastic wrap

Yogurt

The new bud will form from the node that is above the surface, and the new roots will form from the node that is below the surface.

Shoot appears at node.

If you prefer, you can plant your piece of cane vertically, but the new shoot will come out sideways—which doesn't look quite so good. Cover the pot with plastic wrap and set it on the yogurt maker. It will need all the help it can get.

Sideways

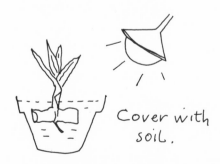

Cover with soil.

As soon as the new shoot appears, cover the stem completely with sandy soil. Remove the pot from the yogurt maker and slowly harden up your plant. It will benefit from the best light in the house and needs a moist soil. Try to approximate the Hawaiian climate, which means that an occasional misting or trip to the shower would be appreciated.

When looking for sugarcane to buy, try to get some that doesn't look old and dried out. Your cutting should come from the center of the stem so that it is as moist as possible. (In other words, start eating from both ends and stop before you reach the middle.)

100

SWEET POTATO

Morning-Glory Family

(Ipomoea batatas)

Water Level

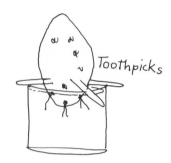

Toothpicks

When you are in the market for a sweet potato to grow rather than eat, look for one that has lots of "eyes," as your vines will appear from them.

Find a jar with a mouth wide enough to take the potato without its falling through. The bottom third of the potato should rest in the water. If you can't find a suitable jar, stick in four toothpicks and balance the potato in the center of the jar.

It takes quite a long time for the first roots to form, so you have to be patient. Once the roots have formed, the vines appear from the eyes.

The sweet-potato vine has a beautiful pale heart-shaped leaf. The stems can grow very long and will benefit from a little judicious pruning.

Fine roots form.

When the roots have completely filled up the glass jar, pot the potato in soil. You can, if you want to, bury the potato completely, even though this means burying the vines also, forcing them to grow through the soil. What I usually do is bury the bottom half that has been growing in water.

As the vines grow longer and longer, they frequently lose some of their bottom leaves; so it is a good idea to find a deep pot and bury your potato halfway down with the top sticking out. As the bottom leaves drop off, you can add more and more soil until the potato is completely buried, along with the lower parts of the vines that have lost their leaves.

Original Level

101

UMBRELLA TREE   *(Schefflera)*   Ginseng Family

This is a very popular plant available in many varieties, each with a different name, which can become confusing. In Australia, where it grows as a tree, its botanical name is *Brassaia actinophylla*. In New Zealand, where it has seven to ten fingers, it is called *Tupidanthus calyptratus*. In India it is called *Schefflera venulosa* and has five to six fingers. There is a new miniature variety available which grows wide rather than tall and has palms with eight shiny dark green fingers.

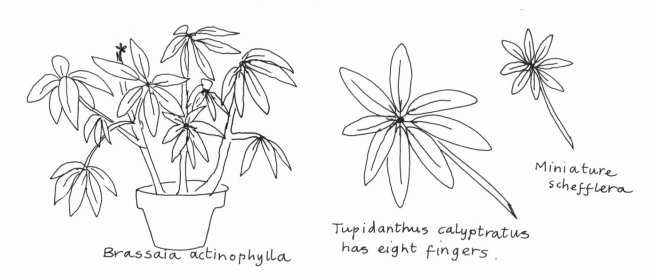

Brassaia actinophylla

Tupidanthus calyptratus
has eight fingers.

Miniature
schefflera

This is one of those plants for which the books all tell you to do one thing, but I find that my plants will grow only if I do exactly the *opposite*. For instance, you are commonly told that scheffleras do not need good light; following this rule, I now have on my upstairs balcony a whole platoon of old soldiers who have lost their lower leaves. However, in the brighter light of outdoors they all put out new growth, which gave me the idea of putting any new scheffleras right in front of my brightest window.

These lovely plants all have a tendency to lose their bottom leaves. This is normally the result of overwatering; but here again, one book tells you that they barely need any water at all, and another tells you to give them a good soaking each time you water.

The secret, dear friends, is to let them dry out completely before rewatering. (When in doubt, consult your "second opinion"—the watering guide.) You can be sure that if your schefflera keeps losing its bottom leaves, although it appears to be bone dry on the surface, it will be sopping wet at the bottom of the pot. Plastic pots have a horrible way of concealing the truth; and as you insert your watering guide, it will read different conditions—"dry, moist, wet"—as it goes down. Wait until the bottom of the pot reads "dry" before rewatering, even if the topsoil looks like a desert.

There are three ways to propagate your schefflera.

Offsets

If you are lucky enough to have a plant that puts out offsets at the soil level, these can be cut off. Clear away a little soil around the base of the offset and try to take a little of the mother's roots with it. Plant it in a small pot of vermiculite, cover it with a greenhouse and set it on the yogurt maker. When roots form (in four to six weeks), take the pot off the yogurt maker, harden up your plant gradually and replant it in the same pot in potting soil.

Offset

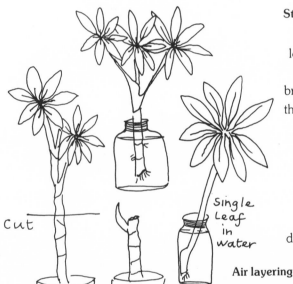

Cut

Tip cutting   New shoot

Single Leaf in water

Stem and leaf cuttings

If you have a young plant that has lost all its lower leaves, you can cut off the top leaves and root the stem in water. You can also root a single leaf, broken off from the main stem; the instructions are the same for both.

Stand your cutting in a bottle of water on a bright windowsill or under a plant light. When the roots reach one to two inches in length, they can be potted in soil. When transferring water-rooted cuttings to soil, be sure to follow the antishock directions given on page 7.

Air layering

If your old plant has lost all its bottom leaves, leaving you with a large expanse of ugly stem, you can air layer the stem. Six inches below the bottom leaves make a cut at an angle of 45 degrees. Put a toothpick into the cut to prevent it from sealing itself shut. Wrap the cut in moist sphagnum moss, and cover the moss in plastic wrap, tied at the top and bottom with Twist-ems. To make sure that the moss does not dry out, add more water with a meat baster as needed. In four to six weeks new roots will form through the moss. The stem can be cut through just below the roots, and the whole root ball planted in potting soil.

Don't throw away the original plant because sometimes it puts out a new shoot just below the stub.

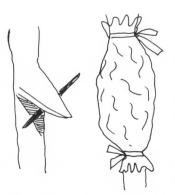

WANDERING JEW   (Tradescantia)   Spiderwort Family

Wandering Jew is the name given to many species of tradescantia, but it is technically the zebrina, a cousin, which is the true Zionist. Wandering Jews are colorful plants with many variations; they have wonderful striped leaves, usually with various shades of purple, green, and white, and some are even furry. Tradescantias, named after John Tradescant, head gardener to Charles I of England, are actually a little more substantial than zebrinas. Their stems are thicker and their leaves are not quite so fragile. They are also called "inch plants."

Tradescantia
albiflora
albo - vittata

thicker
stem

Rooting in water

All forms of wandering Jew can be propagated the same way—very easily—in water. Break off four-inch tip cuttings and root them together in a small bottle of water on a windowsill. They will form roots very quickly, probably within one week. The roots form at the nodes (where the leaves join the stem). When the roots are one to two inches long, you can pot them in soil.

Zebrina
pendula

T. blossfeldiana
'Pussy Ears'

Crock a pot and fill it with potting soil. Take a stick and make holes in the soil into which you can put each cutting. Be very careful when separating their roots. Put in as many cuttings as you can. When the pot is full, water it with a vitamin B_1 solution and put it into a plastic-bag greenhouse for a week. Harden it up, and you have an instant plant.

If you find that the stems of your wandering Jew are growing very thin and breaking easily, bury the tip of each stem under the soil in the pot. It will form new roots under the soil and then push itself from under the soil toward the light, becoming stronger in the process. This can be repeated two or three times, and each time the stem tip comes up for air, it will be thicker. To grow a bushy plant, keep pinching back the tips with your thumb and forefinger. This will force new growth at the soil level. The Wandering Jew is a lovely plant which is easy to propagate, and you will be very happy with it.

104

PROPAGATION BY SEED

Sexual propagation occurs only in plants that have seeds and spores. All the other methods described in this book are asexual and are known as "vegetative propagation."

Growing from seed is time-consuming but rewarding. You will never cease to marvel that the flower you have grown once came from a seed so small that you could barely see it with your naked eye. I think that everyone should grow a plant from seed at least once. It teaches so many things—patience, caring and wonder.

The seed is formed at the base of the flower, in a "pod" which is the ovary. You have probably seen it in a fuchsia when the flower has dropped off; you must have seen it on a rose. That vitamin C you take sometimes comes from rose hips, the "hip" being the berrylike pod that encloses the seeds of the rose.

"Dead-heading" of old blooms is removing these pods. Experimenters have found that if you remove all the dead heads as soon as they have flowered, you will have a much hardier plant. Otherwise, all the energy needed to form flowers will be going into creating seeds. After all, as far as the plant is concerned, its flowers are merely an indication that it is fertile and preparing to make seeds!

If you remove the ripened ovary from a plant and keep it in a closed container, the pod will pop open and the seeds will be inside. At planting time they may germinate—but then again, they may not, because some seeds need a dormant period before germination. If you would like to grow seeds, buy some from a reputable seed grower.

Nurseries that specialize in growing seeds allow their plants to "go to seed," meaning that they are allowed to grow any old way in order to produce offspring and not just to look beautiful. Gardens that have gone to seed are just like people in the same condition—interesting to look at but not very presentable.

Germination

The ideal germinator is a transparent plastic box with a fitted lid. Two holes should be made in the lid and the bottom of the box with an ice pick that has been heated over a flame. This allows for ventilation and drainage. Make up a soil mixture of half sand and half potting soil and fill the bottom of the box to a depth of two inches.

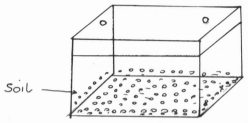

Soil

Transparent plastic box and lid

If you want to grow a lot of plants from seed, you might be better off with a seed box. Seed boxes are available from any plant supplier and are made of wood or plastic. I prefer the wooden boxes, but be sure to wash them out thoroughly with hot, soapy water to which you have added a dash of household bleach. The bleach acts as a fungicide. To be extra careful, you can make up a solution of insecticide and water and spray it over the box.

Seed box

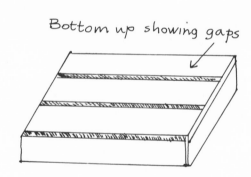

Bottom up showing gaps

Seed boxes have gaps between the bottom slats, which are a nuisance as the soil runs out through the spaces. Either take small pebbles and fill up the gaps, or wet some sphagnum moss and stuff it in between the slats.

Prepare a sandy soil (half soil, half sand) and fill up the seed box, packing it down with the bottom of a spare flowerpot. Take a ruler and make a series of shallow indentations two inches apart. Plant the seeds in the furrows. Try to space the seeds evenly apart; don't put them all in on top of one another. You are supposed to cover the seeds to a "depth equal to three times the diameter of the seed," but as most seeds are barely visible to the naked eye, this is impossible. With a flour sifter sift a fine layer of soil over the seeds until they are covered. As a fungicide, add a finely shredded layer of sphagnum moss.

Box filled with soil and planted with seeds at two-inch intervals

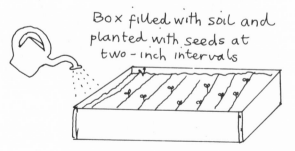

Spray the seeds with a fine mist of water. Be careful not to wash any of them away. Cover the box with a pane of glass or a plastic dry-cleaning bag.

If you have just a few seeds to germinate, you can use any container as long as it has bottom drainage. The bottom half of a plastic-coated milk container will do perfectly, as will a soup can with one or two holes punched in the bottom.

Crock the container with very fine pieces of crocks, or with pebbles to prevent the soil from washing out of the bottom hole when you water. Fill the pot with the same mixture of sandy soil. If your seeds are large enough to handle, try to space them apart from one another. If they are too small to separate, sprinkle them over the surface. Sift a fine layer of soil over them, then add a little sifted sphagnum moss. Water with a fine spray, making sure that the water soaks into the soil. Cover with plastic wrap.

After a couple of weeks, two little leaves will poke their heads up above the soil from each germinating seed. These are the "seed leaves," the cotyledons, which are folded within the seed. The second set of leaves are the true leaves, which will follow a few days later. As soon as they arrive, it is time for "pricking out."

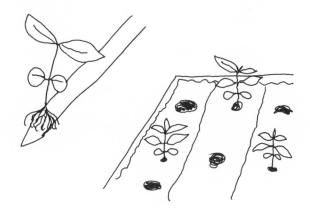

Pricking out

This term refers to the process of transferring the tiny seedlings to their second home, which can be as large as a seed box if you have a lot of seedlings, or a six-inch flowerpot if you have just a few. Fill the box or pot with soil and make a hole for each seedling, spacing the holes at regular intervals over the surface.

Gently grasp the seed leaves and dig up the tiny seedling with its new roots, using a flat thin object—an ice-cream stick is perfect— as a spade. Put the plant quickly into its new home, gently pressing the soil around the roots to hold it firmly. Water with a vitamin B_1 antishock treatment for a week. This removal to its second home can be quite a shock to a tiny seedling, so make a greenhouse for it.

Two-inch pot with jam jar

You can make a greenhouse for a seed box by wedging wire coat hangers into two opposite sides of the box and suspending a plastic dry-cleaning bag over them. Leave a small gap so that a little air can circulate. A too-moist atmosphere would invite the dreaded "damping-off disease," which is a fungus parasite that attacks the seedlings at the soil level.

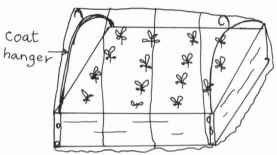

Plastic greenhouse

Coat hanger

After a few days, if you can see that the seedlings are not wilting, they can be hardened up by gradually widening the gap between the bag and the box. The seedlings should stay in their second home for about a month to give them a good root structure. They should receive good light, plus additional "sun" from a plant light if you have one. At this stage, you can use a weak solution of your regular fertilizer, diluted to one-eighth of its usual strength.

Cut into squares like a cake.

Potting seedlings

In a seed box, cut the soil in squares like a cake. Each square of soil containing the plant's roots should be replanted in a four-inch flowerpot. Add additional soil around the sides and bottom to fill the pot.

Stem

Crown

Be sure to notice from where the leaves are growing. If they are growing from the top of the stem, you can bury the roots and stem to any depth so long as the leaves are above the surface. If, however, the leaves are all growing from a crown at the soil level, *be sure to replant them at the same depth.*

So there you have it, one of nature's miracles. And, as a final note, I have it on the highest authority that seeds grow faster on a diet of Bach, with the bass speaker turned up!

CARE OF YOUR MATURE PLANTS

You don't have to go to school to learn how to take care of your plants.
You just have to pay attention to them and try to be sensitive to their needs.

Across the street lives a neighbor who loves her plants. Through her open kitchen door I can
see her washing her plants' leaves, misting them, giving them their daily ration of sunshine. Watching
her, I have often thought to myself, now there's a woman who *really* cares for her plants.

One day we met and she invited me into her house. I don't think I have ever seen such
healthy-looking plants in my life, even at my nursery. There was a hearty dieffenbachia
sharing a pot with a dracaena; when I asked her why she had planted them together, she
said, "Well, the dieffenbachia wasn't doing very well, and it occurred to me that it was
lonely."

Her instincts were correct, even if her reasons weren't. The fact was, the pot was much
too large for the single plant. But when another plant was put in with it to share the root
space, the dieffenbachia immediately stopped producing roots and started producing leaves.
(See Mrs. Parkinson's law, page 113.)

My neighbor is a natural gardener, and whether her green thumb comes from her attention to her plants or from the fact that she breathes carbon dioxide all over them, the result is
that her plants thrive. If you too can learn to think of your plants as living entities with likes
and dislikes, your plants will reward you by flourishing.

To take care of your plants' needs, you must pay attention to their light, water, humidity
and temperature requirements.

LIGHT

As all plants originally grew outdoors, one would imagine that they all needed sunlight.
But this is not true. Tropical plants, growing on the floors or branches of the great forests,
have adjusted to light that is filtered to a perpetual gloom. Bright sunlight would kill them.

A fairly simple rule to follow is that *plants with pale green leaves require more light than
those with dark green leaves.* The amount of light is probably more important to plants than
any other requirement. Plants somehow seem to get by when they are underwatered or
underfed, but put a plant in poor light and it will promptly go into a decline.

Remember what you learned at school: *photosynthesis* is the action of sunlight upon the
green coloring of leaves. This action, utilizing water and minerals applied to their roots,
results in the manufacture of starch and then sugar. Plants, by transforming light, water and
air into food, are true alchemists.

Think of light as your number-one requirement. Light is usually better in the winter when the sun lies lower in the sky and comes further into your rooms. In the summer the sun rides higher and your plants may start "reaching." When plants "reach," they grow tall and spindly, with the internodes (the spaces between the nodes) becoming longer and longer. If this happens, augment the light with some type of plant light. A 150-watt floodlight, fitted into a metal fixture with a clamp, can work wonders on plants that need more light. There is a whole range of wide-spectrum plant lights now available to the indoor gardener that can transform an area once considered too dark for plants into a garden.

TEMPERATURE

Houseplants will grow happily in temperatures between 60 degrees and 80 degrees Fahrenheit. Out of doors, the nightly temperature usually drops *at least* 10 degrees; it is wise to remember this during the winter when the heat is on full blast.

Your plants will grow far healthier if you learn to imitate nature and allow your home to become cooler at night. That 10-degree difference is very important to your plants.

•

It's the warmth of our houses in winter that does our plants in. If the warmth were accompanied by humidity (as in the tropics or a greenhouse), our plants would all flourish. Without humidity they find it hard to survive, so mist your plants more frequently when the heat is on. Soil dries out much faster in a hot, dry atmosphere also, so remember to water your plants more frequently.

WATER

So much depends on the temperature of your room and the amount of light available to your plants that I really hate to give advice about watering. I was once told that it was better to underwater than overwater, which makes sense until you get a really fragile plant. Then that one extra day without water could kill it. But in general you are more likely to kill a plant by overwatering than the reverse.

It's very hard to tell if a plant needs watering just by looking at it, because an "I'm thirsty" droop to one plant can mean just the opposite to its neighbor. (See pages 45 and 54.)

Learning your plants' personal idiosyncrasies is the only way to water them successfully. Certain plants need to be kept constantly moist, whereas others need to dry out in between watering. A watering guide that you stick into the soil—there are several kinds on the market—will at least provide a second opinion.

It is also sensible to buy your plant supplies at the same place and make friends with the expert who sells them to you. My plant consultant, John Lankester, has helped me with all my plant problems, and his knowledge is worth more than one-hundred plant books (with their conflicting advice). I hope you can all find someone like him to help you.

Ice cubes

Ice cubes are a wonderful way to water your hanging plants without getting your armpits wet. They are invaluable, too, for watering pot-bound plants—the ice melts slowly, giving the plant a chance to absorb the water. Don't worry that the ice will freeze your plants because it melts at room temperature.

HUMIDITY

We all keep our houses far too warm, and our plants suffer as a result. Here are some ways to compensate for the lack of humidity.

Spraying and misting

Mist or spray with water at least once a day. This doesn't, as I once read, keep a plant dust-free because, as every woman knows, dust is waterproof! But it does provide the additional humidity that most plants need (with the exception of hairy-leaved plants, which can develop mold if their leaves get wet).

Steam

Have you noticed how plants do so much better in the bathroom? This is because of the steam from the shower and not because they are voyeurs.

And cuttings on the shelf above the kitchen sink invariably root twice as fast—if you do as much washing up as I do.

Plants love steam, so try putting a recalcitrant plant into the shower after you have used it, and notice how it appears to grow more luxuriously. (See page 28.)

Saucers and trays

A simple way to provide humidity is to fill up the saucers or trays that your pots stand in with pebbles. Add water so that the pebbles are half-submerged. The base of your pot stands on dry stones, but the water underneath evaporates slowly, creating humidity around the plants.

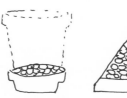 

FERTILIZING

As with watering, some plants need more than others. As a basic rule, once a month I make up a solution of highly concentrated water-soluble plant food, which seems to have the necessary ingredients to keep my plants happy.

For hanging plants, I make up a solution of plant food and freeze it into ice cubes. I use six cubes per plant once a month and no longer wonder if they are getting fed properly. I keep a supply of them in the freezer marked "For Plants, Not Humans."

Dormancy

Most houseplants come from the tropics, where they have a four-month dry season (usually coinciding with our winter), during which, through lack of rain, they have been forced to develop dormancy patterns to survive (like bears who sleep through the winter owing to lack of food). When a plant is in its dormant state, it should barely be watered and not fertilized at all. Follow the rule that you should only fertilize a plant that shows active growth. If you fertilize a dormant plant, you will burn its roots, because only a growing plant can utilize nourishment. We don't eat when sleeping—well, neither do plants.

Plants that grow from tubers, such as cyclamens, caladiums and tuberous begonias, have a definite cycle of growth and rest. As soon as they stop flowering and lose their leaves, they are going into their dormant cycle. This is the time to stop fertilizing completely and cut down on water, little by little, until you are giving them a scant teacup every two weeks—just enough to stop them from shriveling up. This period can last from one to three months. As soon as you notice new growth appearing, you can start watering and feeding once more.

Blooming flowers

Geraniums do a lot better if they are fertilized only during their blooming period. Otherwise, (and I learned the hard way) you will get lots of lovely green leaves and absolutely no flowers. While they are flowering, they can be fed once a month.

Fuchsias, on the other hand, can be fed every one to two weeks during the flowering period; this encourages more flowers. All plants in full bloom need to be fertilized twice as often as at other stages of growth.

Leaching out

A buildup of white crust on the sides of the pot is an indication that you are overfertilizing and the plant is unable to absorb all the minerals. You must "leach out your pot," which means flushing out the salts.

Stand your plant in the bathtub or the sink and water it thoroughly. Allow the water to go through the plant and out of the bottom hole. Repeat this process five times, by which time all the salts will have been flushed out of the soil. As the fertilizer also gets flushed out in the process, give your plant a dose of fertilizer before returning it to your living room.

112

If you live in an area where the water is full of salts, the white crust will build up on your pots whether you fertilize your plants or not. In this case, perhaps you should water your plants only with distilled water.

POTTING UP

This is the term used to indicate that your plant has grown out of its pot and needs a larger one. Plants that need repotting are usually referred to as "pot-bound."

Indications that your plant is pot-bound are: the roots start growing out of the bottom hole; the roots rise to the surface of the soil; when you water your plant, the water runs straight out of the bottom hole, having lifted up the crock with its roots; the water refuses to go down at all, the roots having filled up the entire pot.

Roots →

Plants that are pot-bound should be potted up in pots just *one size larger* than their present pots. You can seriously stunt the growth of a plant by taking it from a small pot and putting it into a large one.

Remember Mrs. Parkinson's law for plants: *Roots expand in direct proportion to the amount of space that is available to them.*

Roots

This means that while your plant's roots are wildly expanding to fill up every inch of newly available space below the surface, they will have no energy left for leaves and flowers above the surface.

Many plants, particularly those in bloom, seem to do better when they are pot-bound. Geraniums are a prime example; mine won't flower at all unless the pot squeezes their roots in like a corset.

HANGING BASKETS

Baskets make a pleasant change from pots and are particularly suitable for plants that hang down, such as fuchsia, rabbit's-foot fern and impatiens. Cuttings make excellent material for filling baskets, as they do not have an extensive root structure and are easy to insert. If you don't have any cuttings, buy the smallest plants you can find from your plant supplier. These usually come in tiny 1½- or 2-inch pots.

Round wire baskets are available in various sizes, the best being twelve inches in diameter. Anything larger requires a lot of soil to fill and becomes very heavy. Baskets are also available in "half-circles"; that is, with a flat back and a round front to hang against a wall.

You can create a "basket" out of a plastic pot eight to ten inches in diameter. Heat an ice pick over a flame until it is hot enough to gouge holes through the plastic. If your cuttings have small roots, make small holes. If you have plants in 1½-inch pots, make the holes 1½ inches in diameter. This is a lovely way to show poinsettias. Make four holes in the pot below the lip and insert one tiny plant into each hole. Put two more plants into the top of the pot, and you will have a lovely plant. The new miniature poinsettias are better for these baskets as they stay compact and bushy.

To prepare a basket

You will need sphagnum moss, plastic bags and soil. Soak the moss in water and wring it out. Line the inside of the basket with the moss. Use cut-up pieces of picture wire to secure the moss to the basket in three or four places so that it won't slip. Put two inches of soil into the bottom of a large plastic bag and place the bag on top of the moss in the wire basket, cutting the top down to fit if necessary. Using a plastic bag as a liner prevents the moss and soil from drying out too quickly.

With a sharp pair of scissors or a screwdriver punch a hole near the bottom of the basket through the moss and the plastic bag. Insert a rooted cutting (or small plant), roots first, through this hole. Try not to damage the roots. Add more soil to the plastic liner, pressing it down gently to hold the cutting in place.

Continue to add cuttings in this manner, going around the basket from the bottom up. Cuttings should be three or four inches apart, evenly spaced. As you put in each layer, add a layer of soil to hold them in place. When you reach the top, put one or two cuttings in upright. This is a marvelous way to get a mature-looking plant from cuttings.

114

VACATION TIME

If you're going to be away for no more than two weeks, you can make a bathtub greenhouse and save yourself the trouble of arranging for someone to come in and water the plants while you're away.

Buy a large transparent plastic groundsheet from a hardware store. Open it up and lay it lengthwise in the middle of the bathtub. Place a week's supply of newspapers on the plastic sheet and water them thoroughly. Now put all your plants on the newspapers and water *them*.

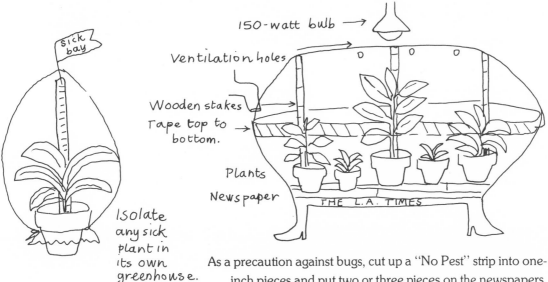

sick bay

Isolate any sick plant in its own greenhouse.

150-watt bulb →

Ventilation holes

Wooden stakes
Tape top to bottom.

Plants

Newspaper

THE L.A. TIMES

As a precaution against bugs, cut up a "No Pest" strip into one-inch pieces and put two or three pieces on the newspapers.

Put stakes into the pots at either end and in the middle of the tub; they will act as a frame to keep the plastic sheet from touching the leaves. Reach over your plants and pick up one end of the plastic sheet, bringing it forward to meet the other side. Trim off the excess plastic, leaving just enough for both edges to overlap. Tape the long side to the edge of the bathtub, then tape the short sides closed. This will give you an oblong package the size of your bathtub. Get a sharp pair of scissors and make three holes, an inch in diameter, in the top of the plastic to allow for some ventilation; this will keep your plants from growing moldy.

Buy a 150-watt floodlight and screw it into the overhead light socket. Leave it on all the time.

When you return from your trip, you are going to be simply amazed at how well your plants are doing. Don't forget to harden them up over a period of one or two days; otherwise, the change of atmosphere will kill them. I hope you have another bathtub or a friendly neighbor. . . .

If one of your plants is sick, put it into its own plastic-bag greenhouse away from the others.

This is probably a far safer way of keeping your plants alive than depending on a too-willing neighbor who, in her anxiety to take good care of your plants, may end up by drowning them.

SOURCES

I would like to thank John Lankester for his help. His knowledge of plants was more valuable to me than all the books I read.

Baylis, Maggie. *House Plants for the Purple Thumb.* San Francisco: One Hundred One Productions, 1973.

Better Homes & Gardens House Plants. 2nd ed. Des Moines: Better Homes & Gardens, 1971.

Compton, Joan. *House Plants.* Bantam Nature Guide, Knowledge Through Color Series, No. 44. New York: Bantam, 1973.

Cruso, Thalassa. *Making Things Grow.* New York: Alfred A. Knopf, 1971.

Elbert, George and Virginie. *Flowers That Really Bloom Indoors.* New York: Simon and Schuster, 1974.

Free, Montague. *Plant Propagation in Pictures.* New York: American Garden Guild, 1957.

Graf, Alfred B., ed. *Exotica III: Pictorial Encyclopedia of Exotic Plants.* Rev. ed. New York: Scribner, 1974.

Holmes, Sandra. *Flowers of the World,* Bantam Nature Guide, Knowledge Through Color Series, No. 51. New York: Bantam, 1974.

Hottes, Alfred C. *Garden Facts and Fancies.* New York: Dodd Mead & Co., 1949.

House Plants: A Handbook. Brooklyn, N.Y.: Brooklyn Botanic Garden, 1974.

Kranz, Frederick H. and Jacqueline L. *Gardening Indoors Under Lights.* New York: Viking, 1971.

Langer, Richard W. *The After-Dinner Gardening Book.* New York: Macmillan, 1974.

Loewer, H. Peter. *The Indoor Water Gardener's How-to Handbook.* New York: Popular Library, 1974.

Lucas, Richard. *Nature's Medicines.* North Hollywood, Calif.: Wilshire Book Co., 1973.

McDonald, Elvin. *The World Book of House Plants.* New York: Popular Library, 1972.

Morley, Brian D. *Wild Flowers of the World.* New York: Putnam, 1970.

Nehrling, Arno and Irene. *Propagating House Plants.* Great Neck, N.Y.: Hearthside Press, 1971.

Nicholls, Richard. *The Plant Doctor.* Philadelphia: Running Press, 1975.

Perry, Frances, ed. *Flowers of the World.* New York: Crown Publishers, 1972.

Sunset Editors. *How to Grow House Plants.* Menlo Park, Calif.: Lane Magazine & Book Co., 1974.

————. *Sunset Western Garden Book.* Rev. ed. Menlo Park, Calif.: Lane Magazine & Book Co., 1967.

Taylor, Norman, ed. *Encyclopedia of Gardening.* Rev. ed. Boston: Houghton Mifflin, 1961.

Tompkins, Peter, and Christopher Bird. *The Secret Life of Plants.* New York: Harper & Row, 1973.

Whittle, Tyler. *The Plant Hunters.* London: William Heinemann Ltd., 1970.

INDEX

118